PACIFIC
PORTRAITS

*The People Behind the Scenes
at Pacific University*

VOLUME THREE

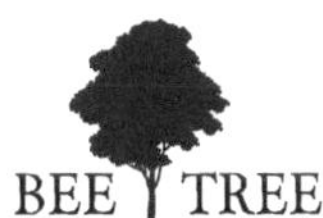

BEE TREE

PACIFIC UNIVERSITY LIBRARIES
Forest Grove, Oregon

Pacific Portraits: The People Behind the Scenes at Pacific University (Volume Three)

Photographs by Macie Akai, Tanner Boyle, Michelle Brown, Cody Burkhart, La'imana Grace,
Ellie Parker, Alyssa Pinter, and Dominic Sampaulesi.

Essays by Sophia Backus, Shelby Cokeley, Avery Kester, Patrick Lagier, Angel Martinez Rojas,
Rachel Savini, Kimberly Su, Julia Thomson, Stephanie Vanschijndel, and Ellie Whitlock.

Interior layout by Michael Arakawa, Sophia Backus, Holly Bartholomew, Jay Bilodeaux, Tanner Boyle,
Tyler Brown, Darcy Christoffersen, Harrison Clifford, Shelby Cokeley, Abby Godsil, Sebastian Herr,
Benjamin Hopwood, Hannah Hulse, Maddison Kellas, Aidan Lannom, Kayla Luttringer,
Haley McKinnon, Tessa Nelson, Luke Olson, Hunter Peterson, Jessica Poluhowich, Chris Shoffner,
Hannah Sites, Stephanie Vanschijndel, Sara Villegas, Erika Vives, and Bobby Ulrich.
Original cover and interior design by Emily Coats

Published by Pacific University Libraries 2017

ISBN-13 978-1-945398-85-8

Pacific University Libraries
2043 College Way
Forest Grove, Oregon 97116

www.pacificu.edu/libraries

Published in the United States of America

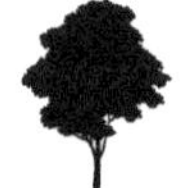

Bee Tree Books
An imprint of the Pacific University Libraries

*Our treasure lies in the beehive of our knowledge. We are perpetually on the way thither, being by nature [...]
honey gatherers of the mind.*
Friedrich Nietzsche

The "Bee Tree", an iconic ivy-covered tree that stood on the Pacific University campus for many years, was
already old and hollow when pioneer Tabitha Brown arrived in Oregon in 1846. Mrs. Brown started a home
for orphans that would grow into Pacific University. According to the Forest Grove *News-Times*, the tree was
"said to have housed a swarm of bees who furnished the little old lady with honey which she sold to buy
provisions for her orphan children."

ACKNOWLEDGMENTS

This project could not have successfully launched without the collective and sustained effort of faculty, staff, and students. They include Jim Flory and his photography students, Darlene Pagán and the writers in creative nonfiction, and Emily Coats at the helm, directing the project early on and working with her students in media arts in the final stages of design and printing. While a number of students doubled up on responsibilities, we owe Shelby Cokeley an extra measure of gratitude for jumping in to save the day so close to the deadline. The staff profiled within the pages of this book were key to its completion and their flexibility and willingness to share is deeply appreciated. We are especially grateful to Johanna Meetz and the library staff around the publication of this book through Bee Tree Press. Thank you one and all.

"It's just amazing to watch them grow. I knew them when they were sophomores and they had these little nuggets of creativity, and now they've just grown so much. It's wonderful to see what they can do."
—REBECCA ALLEN, *Theatre Production Assistant, Manager of Media Art Student Production Services*

"Being a graphic artist is really great because you get to be creative."
—ALEX BELL, *Graphic Designer*

"Helping the community have more access to the arts is really important to me! Especially for children since they are getting less in schools now."
—DANA EYTZEN, *Office Associate and International Admission Assistant*

"I don't get to interact with students nearly as much as I did before. But I feel like the behind the scenes work I do is important to help students even if they don't realize it."
—CLAIRE GADBOIS, *Associate Registrar*

"It's a great joy to have students who have gone on to graduate and still be able to rekindle a conversation with them."
—BRIAN O'DRISCOLL, *Director of the Career Development Center*

"It changed my life, transformed it. More than my degree."
—SAM MORRISON, *Assistant Director of Outdoor Pursuits*

"I am a little bit of everything because everything should have equity."
—NARCEDALIA RODRIGUEZ, *Executive Director of Equity, Diversity and Inclusion*

"My heart is with the transfer students."
—MIKE SHINGLE, *Academic Advisor*

"My heart is on the field…I just can't leave it."
—LIZ YANDALL, *Head Softball Coach*

CONTENTS

FOREWORD

One terrific aspect of a good story is that it often includes surprises, whether because the story turns in a direction we never expect, or leads us into imagined worlds, or transforms a character in an unpredictable way. All of the individuals profiled in these pages reveal surprises, large and small—perhaps not the kind we might associate with a plot driven story, but surprises nonetheless because while we see these individuals sometimes on a daily basis, how much do we really know about them outside of their job descriptions?

We might pass such individuals on campus, ask questions about courses and transfer equivalents, or sign up for an outdoor adventure, or see someone on a baseball field at a practice without ever even knowing a first name. It's a function of our busy lives and theirs, and it's an amazing feat to take a moment and meet people we assumed we knew or people we've only seen and never met.

Our hope is that these stories invite you into the lives of Pacific staff who work behind the scenes but have rich and full lives we often know very little about. In these pages, you'll witness a blueberry fight, a softball practice, and a white water rafting trip.

In the process of these mini-adventures, you will recognize how wide and far the net reaches that encompasses a wide range of individuals we call members of the Pacific family. But in every case, no matter what the titles are of the individuals profiled in these pages, it's clear they work with passion and dedication and that they enjoy the vital work they do to further the mission of the college and support the success of students. These real life characters are full of surprises.

Welcome,
Darlene Pagán, Professor of English
Jim Flory, Assistant Professor of Art
Emily Coats, Instructor of Media Arts

REBECCA ALLEN

narrative by Avery Kester
photographs by Dominic Sampaulesi

On entering Rebecca Allen's office in the second floor of Warner Hall, I notice she has rearranged her furniture. I have visited her office many times before. She tells me she wants her desk to face the walkway through her office because she doesn't like when people sit across the desk from her. She would rather people sit next to her, which feels less stuffy and allows her to show them what she's working on. When I come to see her, she's working on a mock-up of the poster for the Fall Theatre show, Hide. It's the beginnings of what will eventually become a scene of a destroyed cafe, but so far it only has a table on its side.

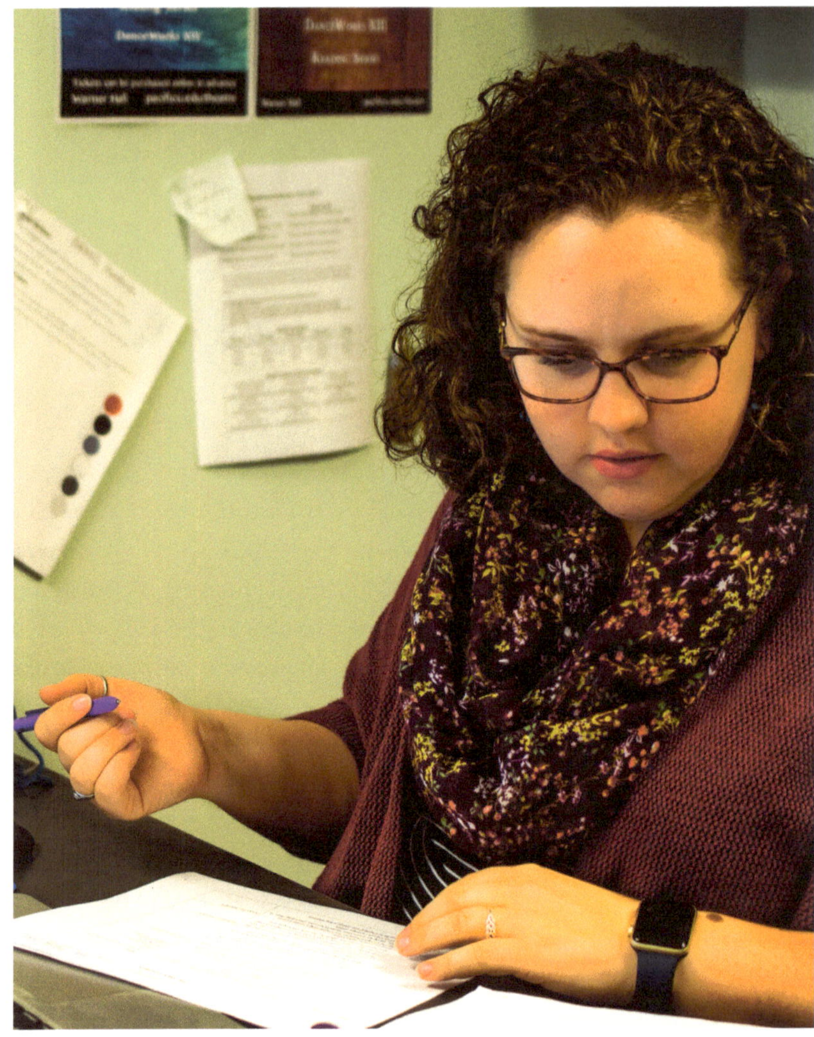

Since Rebecca started working as the Production Assistant for the Theatre Department in the fall of 2015, she has designed the posters for every main stage show that the theatre department has produced. It was in the fall of 2015 when the theatre was putting on SMASH! when I first met Rebecca, and that was also the first show she worked on for the department. We have worked together during Dance Slow Decades, The Good Woman of Setzuan, and several other productions. Lately, the posters she has been making for those shows have become more graphically inclined, moving away from her photography background.

When she started at Pacific University, Rebecca didn't have any graphic design experience. "I actually learned how to use Photoshop about two weeks before I started my job here." Even though she works for the Theatre department now, she studied English while she was in school. She reflects on her time at Portland Community College as well as going to school at Pacific. "Originally I thought I was going to be a writer, but now I'm hoping to eventually be Liz Tavares (an English professor here at Pacific); I want to teach Shakespeare, and maybe a creative writing class or two."

Her stapler matches the color of the wall exactly, the same seafoam green, with paper clips and baskets in that color as well. "I actually bought these things before I saw

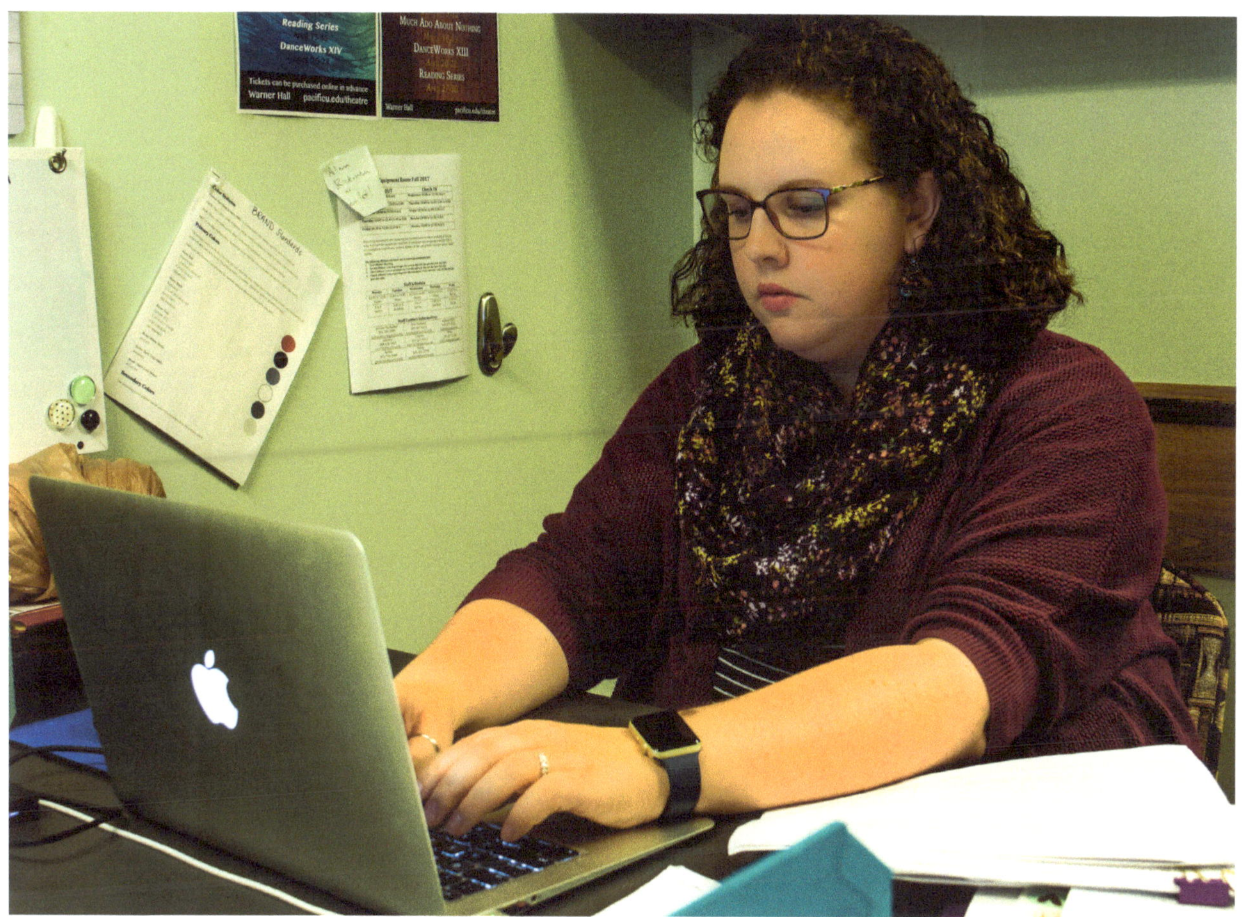

the office and didn't realize it was matching so perfectly." To combat that matchy-matchy aesthetic, she bought some darker teal and purple things, creating a more complete color-scape. There is a pot of faux-purple flowers to complete her desk. I ask her if the flowers are fake, she laughs and explains to me that she doesn't want to be responsible for taking care of real flowers. As the Production Assistant for the Theatre Department, the Manager of MAPS, the Media Arts Production Services, and the person in charge of renting Media equipment out, she doesn't have time to water real flowers.

When I ask her how on Earth she balances her time with all her jobs, she giggles and tells me that the students help her out a lot. They're her favorite part of her Media Arts work. Her eyes glimmer when she discusses how she loves to work with them. "It's just amazing to watch them grow, I knew them when they were sophomores and they had these little nugget of creativity, and now they've just grown so much. It's wonderful to see what they can do." She loves her job in the theatre because it's her creative outlet. Having a balance between a job in which she gets to be the

> "It's just amazing to watch them grow, I knew them when they were sophomores and they had these little nuggets of creativity, and now they've just grown so much."

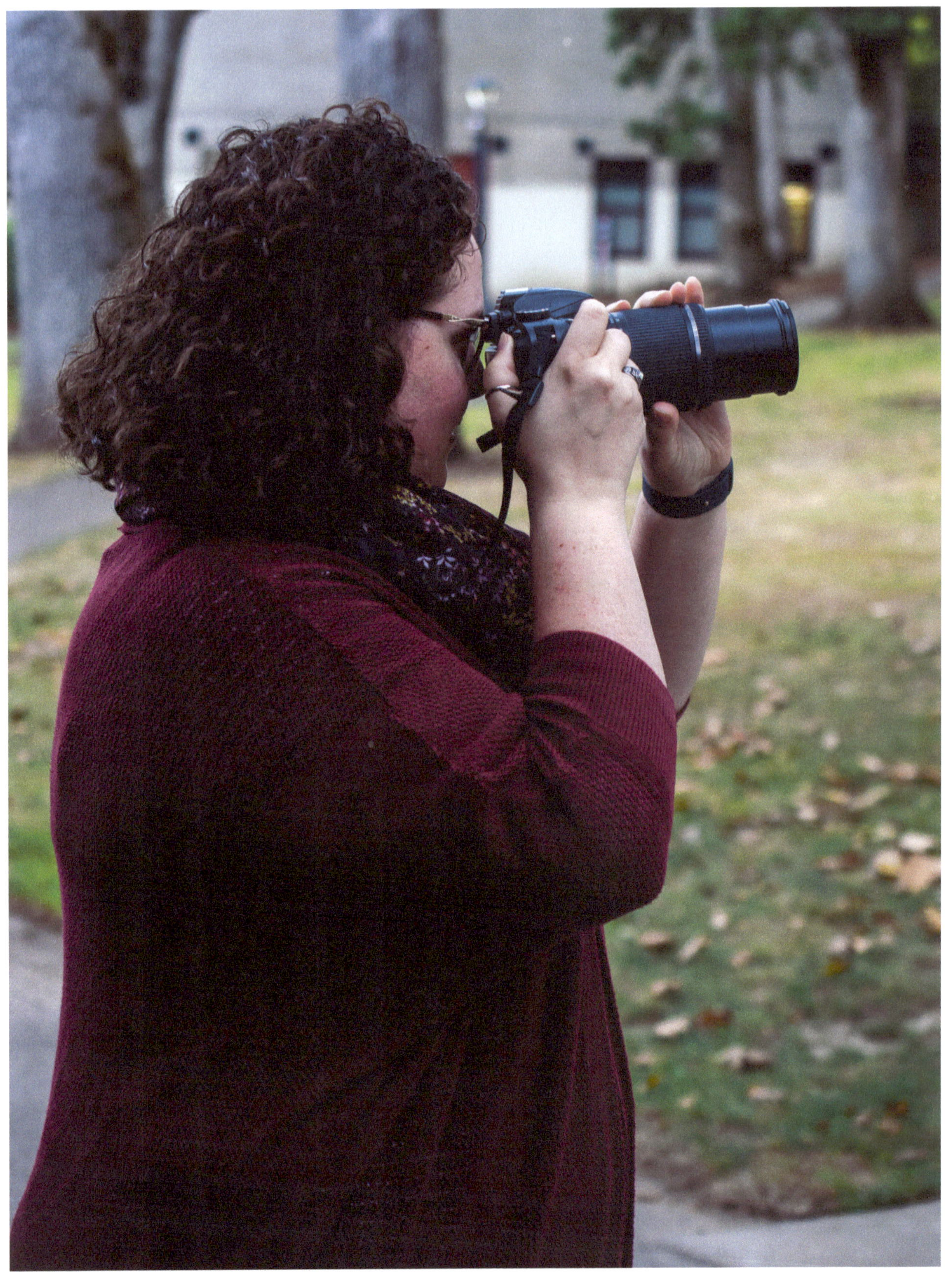

Rebecca Allen | *The People Behind the Scenes of Pacific University*

creative source and a job in which she gets to help students realize their own creative potential is great for Rebecca. She tells me that she's always been an artistically driven person, especially in writing.

Reflecting on her own creative work, she tells me, "There's a lot of very angst-filled writings from my Middle School years." She has a binder full of old poems, and the fonts are color-coded. Different fonts for different themes, different colors for emotions, so she definitely can keep track of which poem is which. While her angst did not follow her to her college writing, her commitment to emotional truth and pushing the boundaries of conventional storytelling did. She describes a piece she wrote while studying at Pacific, "My story in Advanced (Creative Fiction) was about a woman who found out she had terminal Cervical Cancer, and she decided to go through her, what she called her 'fuck-it list', it's like a bucket list. And the last thing that she was going to do was become a porn star. She felt weird about a company making money off of her so she became a cam-model. And her schtick was doing her show while reading classic literature."

While Rebecca likes to push the boundaries with her writing, her real passion comes from helping others discover their creative potential. As she moves forward, Rebecca is applying to several Graduate level programs so she can continue on her own learning path, and eventually become a teacher. Getting the chance to watch her students grow and come into their own is what Rebecca loves about her work now, and it is what makes her want to become a teacher.

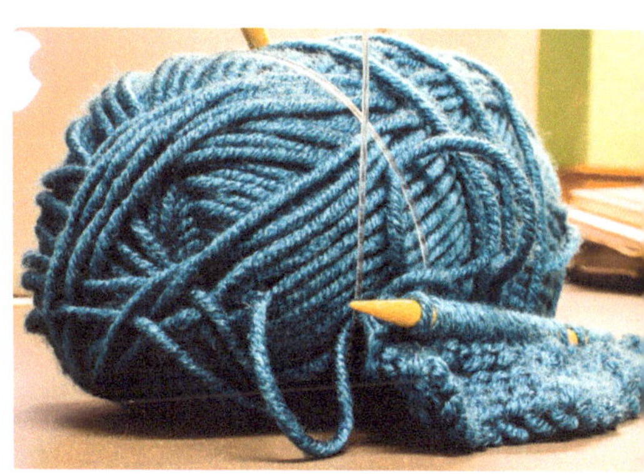

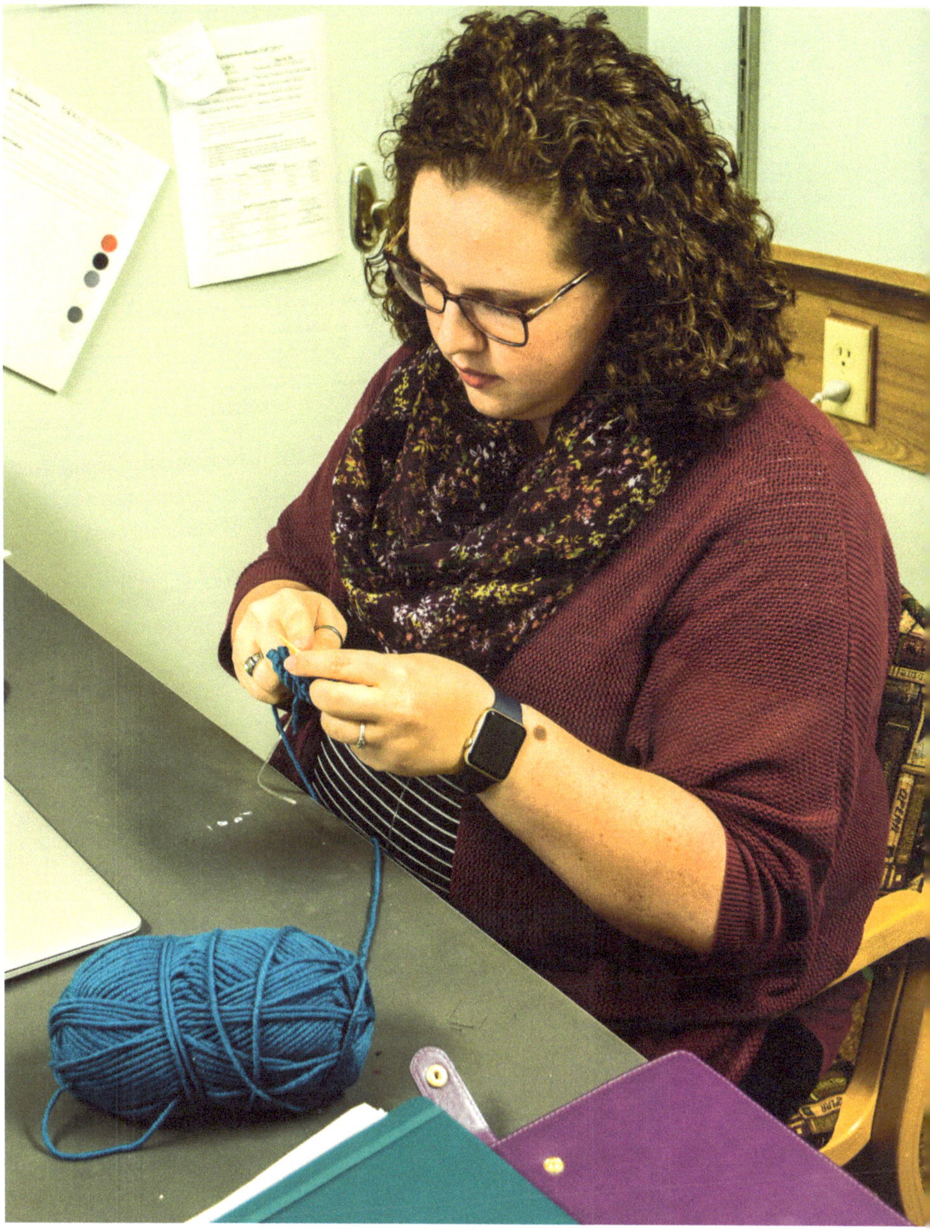

ALEX BELL

narrative by Stephanie van Schijndel
photographs by Alyssa Pinter

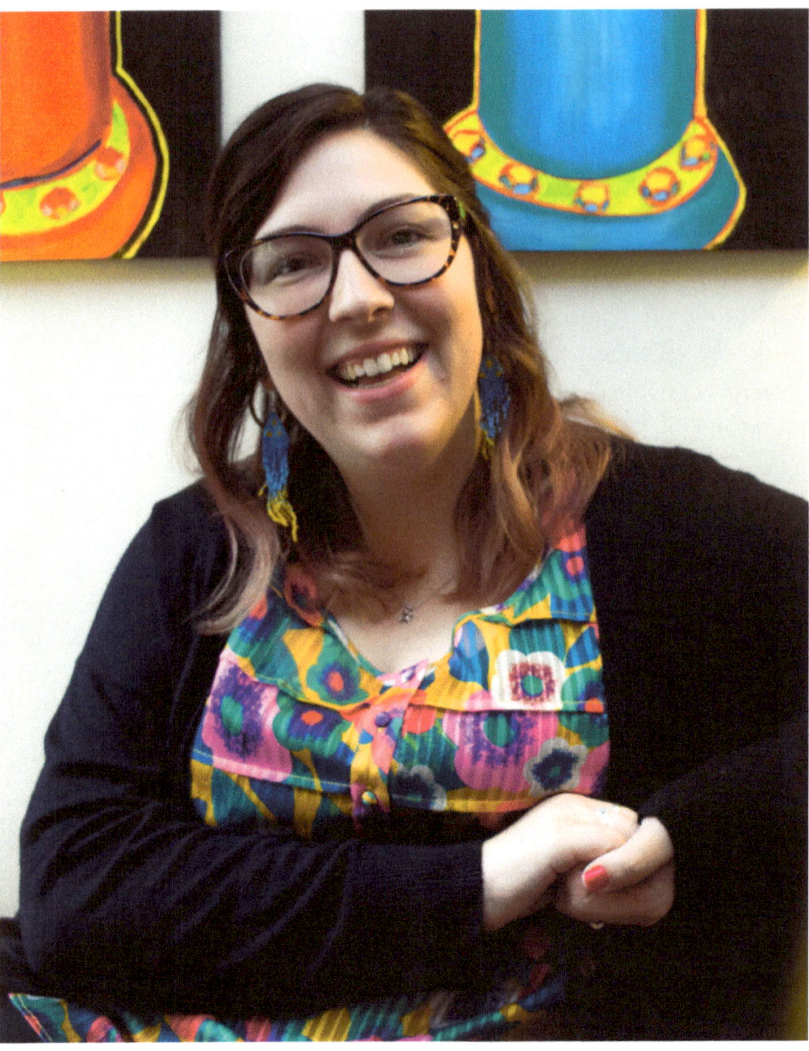

Alex Bell's workspace is in the back corner of the Marketing and Communications office in Scott Hall. Once the door closes, you're in a completely different setting. Little potted plants sit on every flat surface, from shelves, tables, and even room dividers. Colorful paintings hang on every wall. One in particular, of a pink man sitting happily in his green and yellow backdrop, watches the office from the back wall. The workspace itself is tidy and open, with lots of room on the center desk for large projects. It's dark. And quiet. You might wonder if you're in the right place.

Way in the back, three designers huddle round a computer, going over their latest project. Alex's coworkers are Adam, a photographer, and Joyce, an assistant graphic designer, who both stand beside Alex. They're all smiles when I enter the room. Alex's desk is to the right, along the wall of colourful chairs and bookshelves. A large window is at the back of her workspace, behind her desk. Artificial light is less welcome. "Yeah, we like it dim. Fluorescent lights are very

hard to work under." She wears a bright shirt of abstract flowers under a black cardigan, dangling earrings made of small beads that look like blue and yellow jellyfish, and thick socks on with her comfy clogs.

"Being a graphic artist is really great because you get to be creative." Alex has worked at Pacific for four years as a graphic designer. Her passion for design began when she was just a kid, which gave her plenty of practice on her way to becoming a

professional illustrator. Her drawings and paintings are inspired by the environment, as she likes to draw botanical and abstract shapes. On her Instagram is a collection of bright designs, floral patterns and smiling faces of light primary colors. Her work reflects the day to day emotion spoken through expressionism, a subtle yet powerful perception of sweetness regarding the world around her. She'll often find something on her walks to bring home with her to draw,

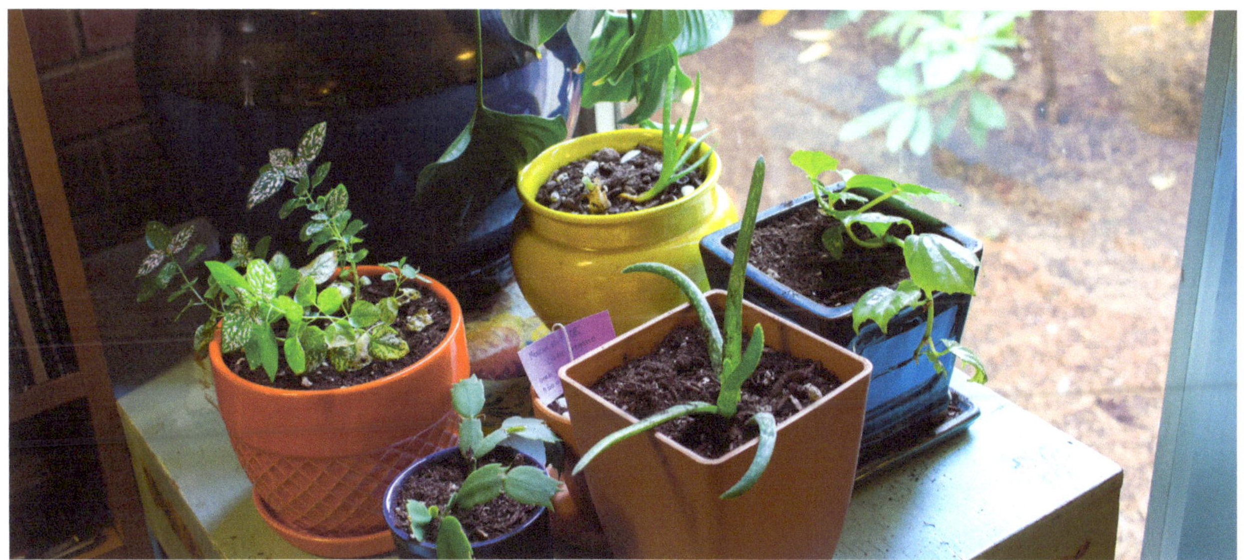

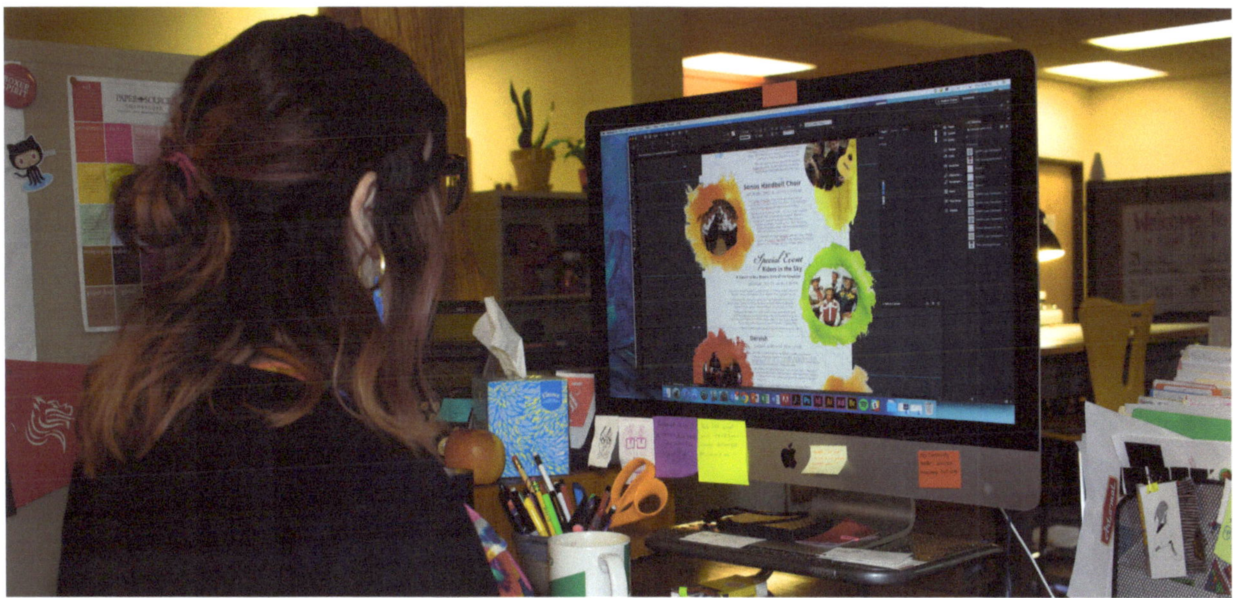

whether she's at the Gorge, on the Rock Creek trail, or on the beach, there is stimulus all around her. Even on campus she finds things to incorporate in her art.

Once a week, Alex attends Boxer Boot Camp, which is a program to help students majoring in physical education gain personal trainer experience. The program also helps with individual wellness and fitness goals. Students and staff are paired in groups of two, and they hike the campus together. For Alex, it's a great excuse to get out of the office, because she's both outside and helping students.

"People is why I work at Pacific." Alex especially likes helping students reach their full artistic potential. Helping an intern with an art show, for example, requires an understanding of the artist and what they wish to present to their audience. Constructing a visually pleasing array of artwork is nothing new to

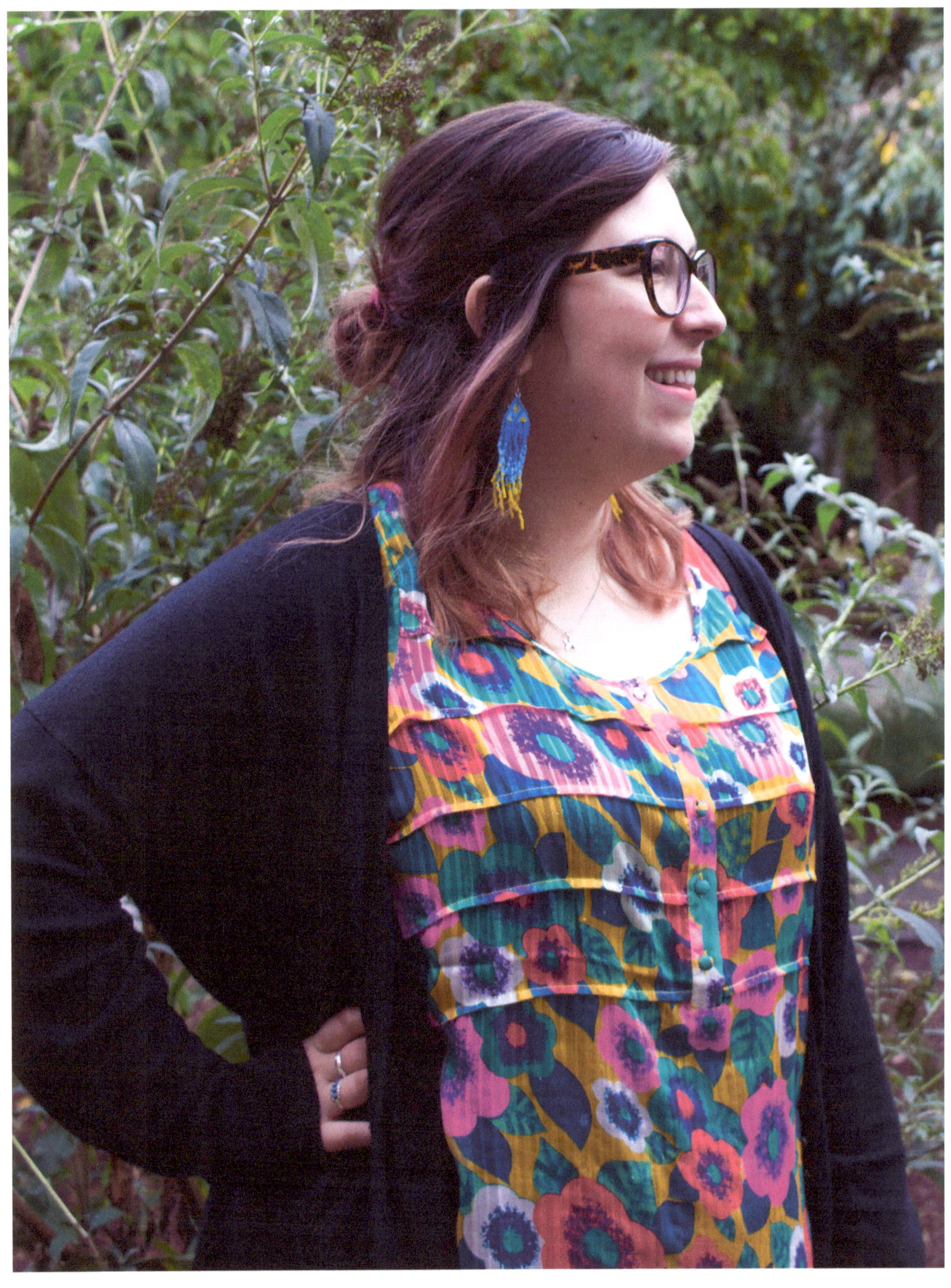

Alex Bell | *The People Behind the Scenes of Pacific University*

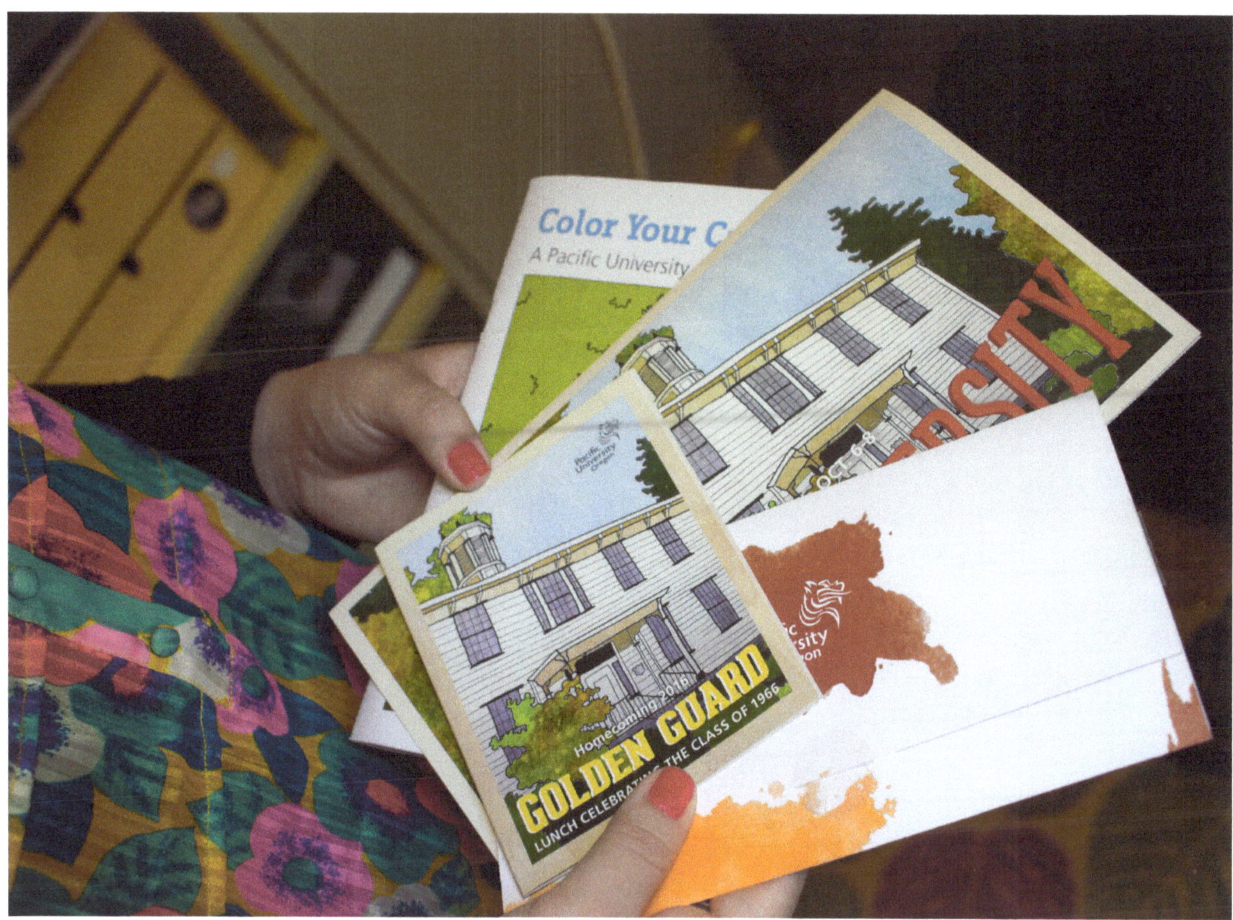

Alex. She shares her knowledge with interns on which pieces to display and how to arrange them. Seeing the finished product of students' hard work is definitely worth it. "It makes me so proud."

As Alex poses for another picture, concentrated more on posture and less on emotion, Joyce comes up behind the photographer with an image of a kitten and catches her off guard. Alex giggles, "We're a cat office for sure." Joyce then shows Adam at his desk, and laughter fills the office. Alex has a cat of her own, a chubby tabby cat named Pretzel. Getting back on topic, she puts her red nail polished hands on her hips, "This [pose] feels very Instagram." Alex sees herself as a composer, orchestrating color and shape to create her designs, so she prefers being behind the camera. She claims it's far more interesting than being in front of it.

As a designer and lover of art, Alex has her own professional website, where she's made a portfolio of her designs, illustrations, and paintings. On ABELL DESIGNS, you'll find special event collateral for Pacific: Homecoming event schedules, School of Healthcare Administration and Leadership brochures, and Pacific University Legends invitations. Along with works for Pacific, Alex has a collection of earthy greeting cards with more examples of her illustrations and paintings—little messages like hey you, surrounded by deep green leaves and neutral blue flowers. Alex's love for the outdoors is reflected in her art, and her dedication to students and staff is evident in the precision of her Pacific designs. A composer, illustrator, cat lover, and graphic designer, Alex Bell is a devoted staff member of the university.

DANA EYTZEN

narrative by Ellie Whitlock
photographs by Ellie Parker

OF ALL THE OFFICES ON CAMPUS, Knight Hall seems quietist. Cozy and homey, the old Victorian house is where the Undergraduate Admissions offices are located. Going down the hall towards the back you might not imagine there is an office tucked away in the back corner. Dana Eytzen sits here at her desk looking at the computer screens in her small but pleasant office. A bulletin board of photos shows off her photography skills with pictures of her animals and family.

When asked what she does at school, she would say she is an "Office Associate International Admission Assistant". She processes the incoming applications for all the undergraduate students which include applications, transcripts, and anything else related to when a student applies to Pacific. She also takes care of all the financial deposits, processes them, and readies the student files for the different departments across campus, like the Registrar and Advising. When asked what she likes to do in her free time, Dana says photography.

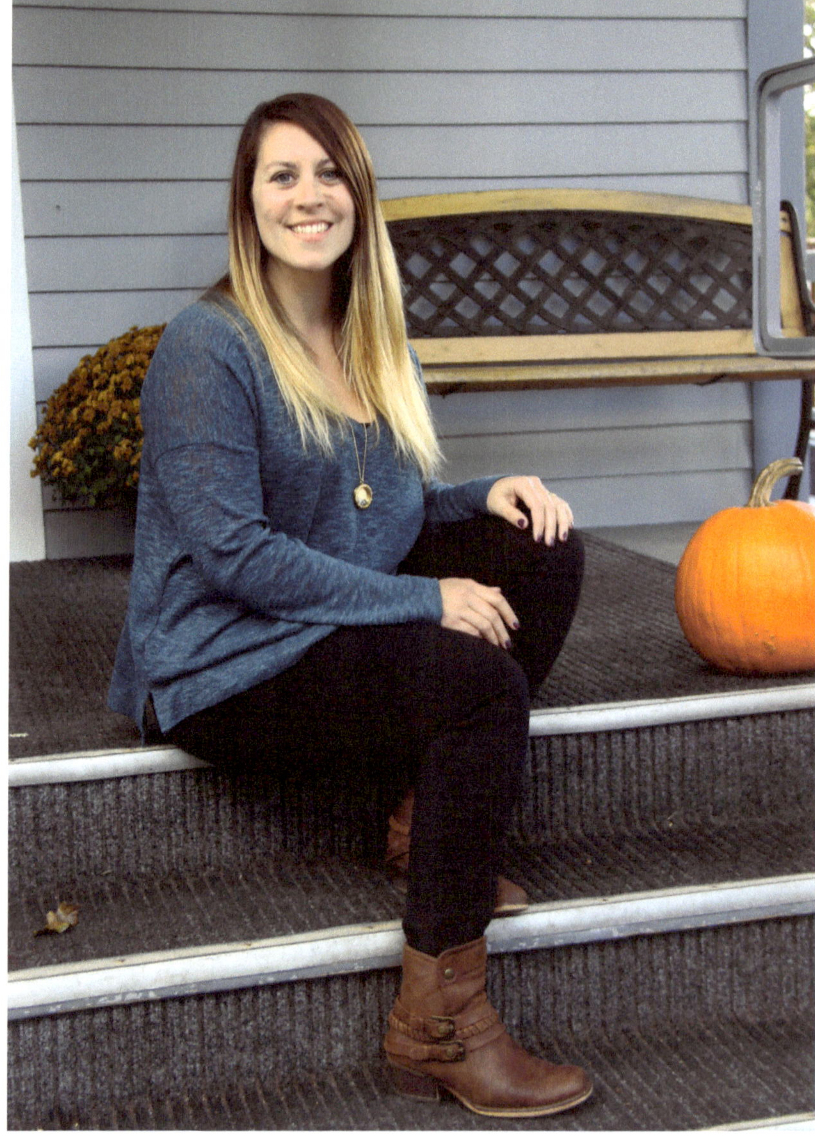

Photography is her main hobby. She likes to photograph nature, take portraits, and she used to photograph a couple of weddings a year. Other than photography, Dana likes to garden, planting just about anything she can find that will grow in the area. She mostly grows the normal vegetables, such as squash, carrots, tomatoes, corn, peppers, artichoke, and broccoli. She also grows basil and other herbs as well as raspberries, blueberries, and roses. "I think the most interesting thing I grew were brussel sprouts, but they got really buggy so I let my goats eat them." Her two goats, Cocoa and Ellie, weigh about 50 lbs each. "Ellie is the more friendly of the two. She likes to be pet, but Cocoa is like, "Eehh, you can stand near me but I don't think I want you to touch me.'"

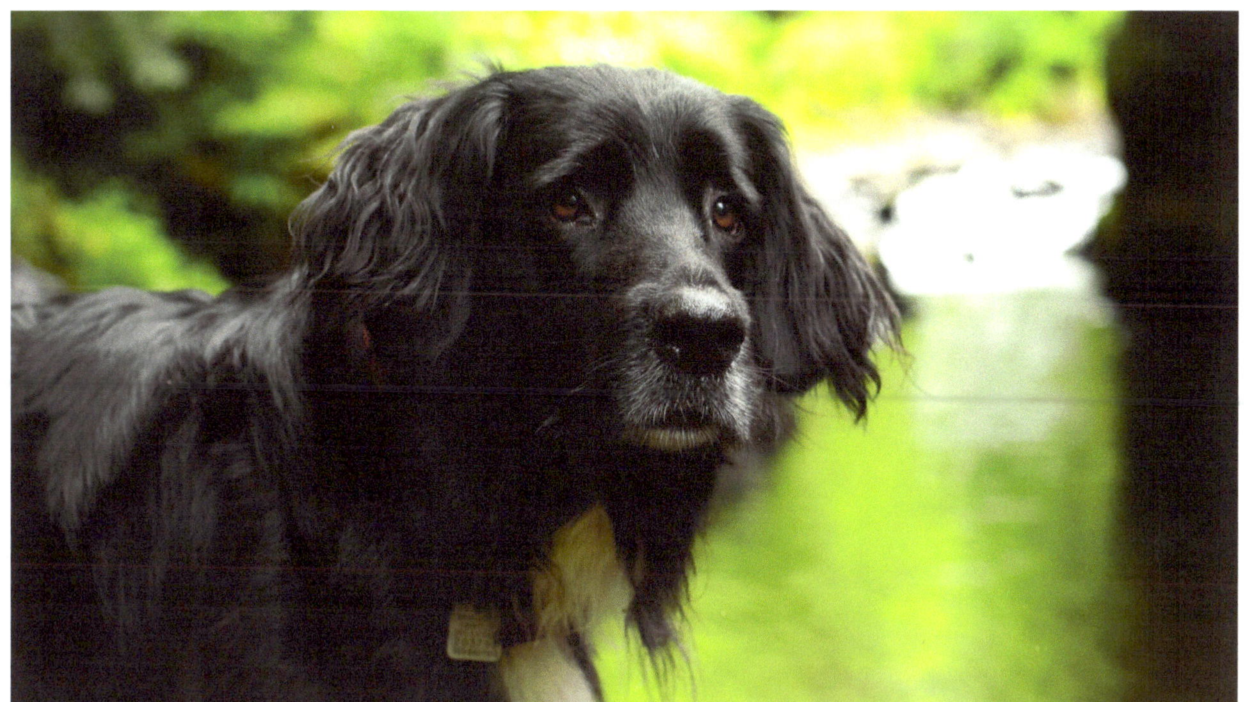

Since she grew up on a farm, she has the goats mostly to eat the blackberry bushes that tend to take over. "Eventually I'd like to either breed my goats or get a few more." She grew up on the farm in Gaston with her parents, and after her grandfather passed away, Dana, her mom and dad, and her grandmother all lived in the four houses that are on the property. Her grandmother lived in one, her dad in another, her mom in a third, and Dana herself in the fourth. The farm is being leased to a farmer who grows wheat and clover. She now lives with her husband in Verboort.

Dana's favorite things about Pacific are the people and the community and during the Pacesetters competition (which offers high school

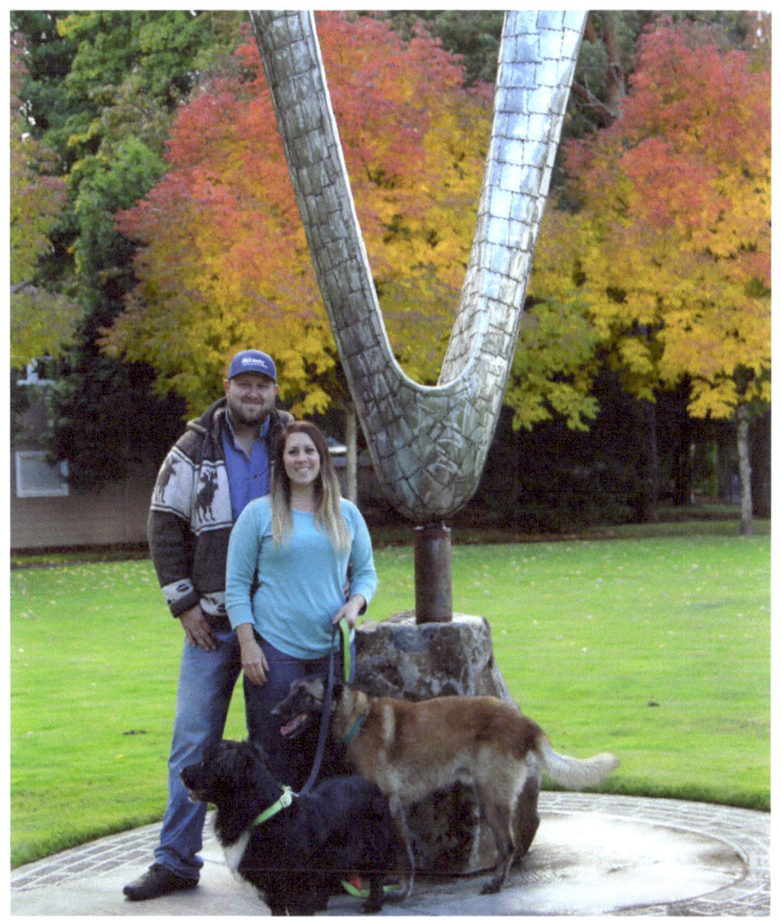

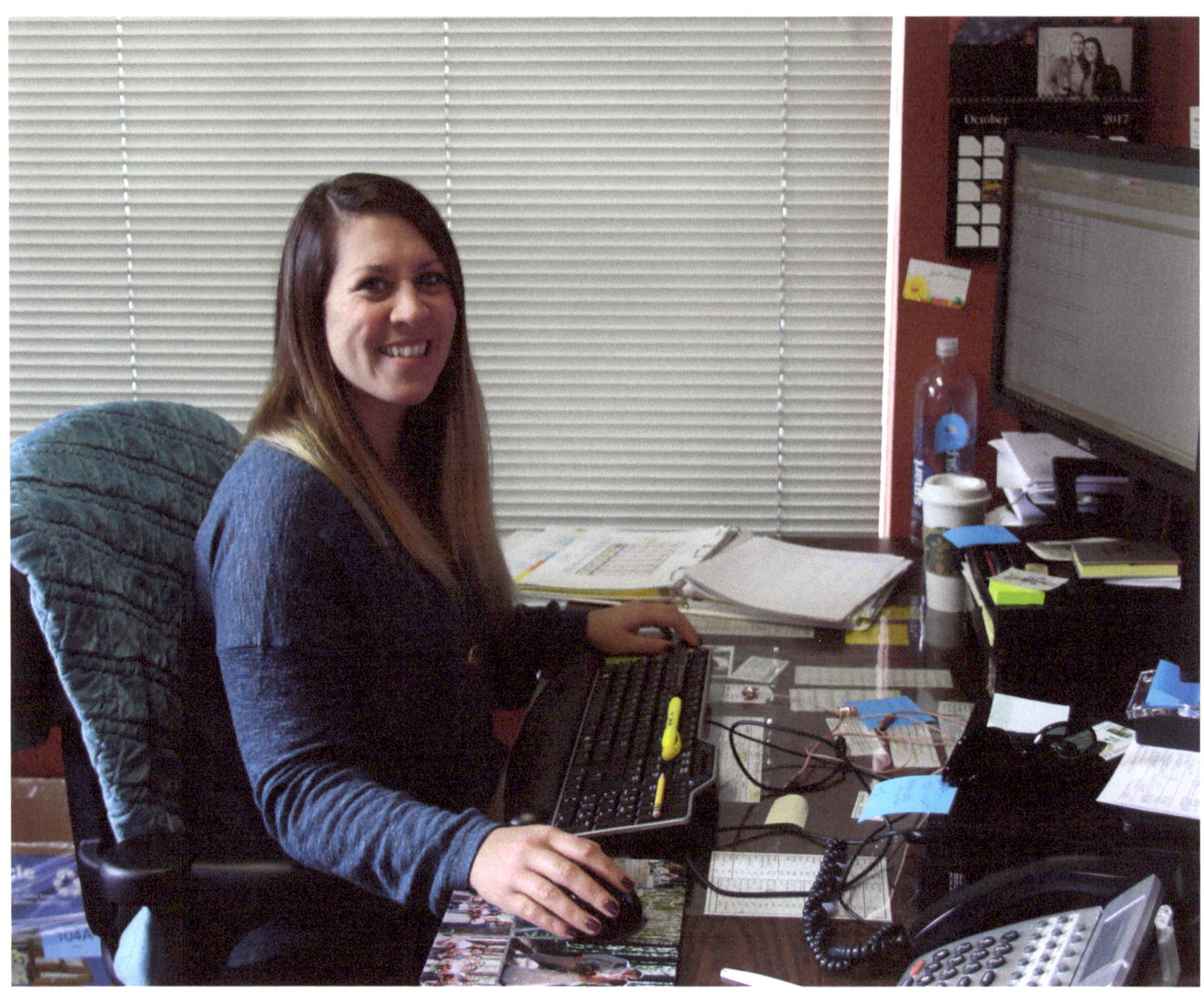

seniors the chance to take an exam for the chance to earn one of two full tuition scholarships), she likes to be able to match the applications to the faces of the students who come to visit campus for the competition.

Outside of school, Dana likes to go camping and hiking during the summer, as well as hanging out with her godsons; Lucas and Jamison. "Ian [her husband] and I like to try new restaurants and breweries…We also like to host small get-togethers or BBQ's at our house." Not only does Dana like being outdoors, she is also the Chair of the Forest Grove Public Arts Commission. "Helping the community to have more access to the arts is really important to me! Especially for children, since they are getting less in schools now."

"Helping the community to have more access to the arts is really important to me."

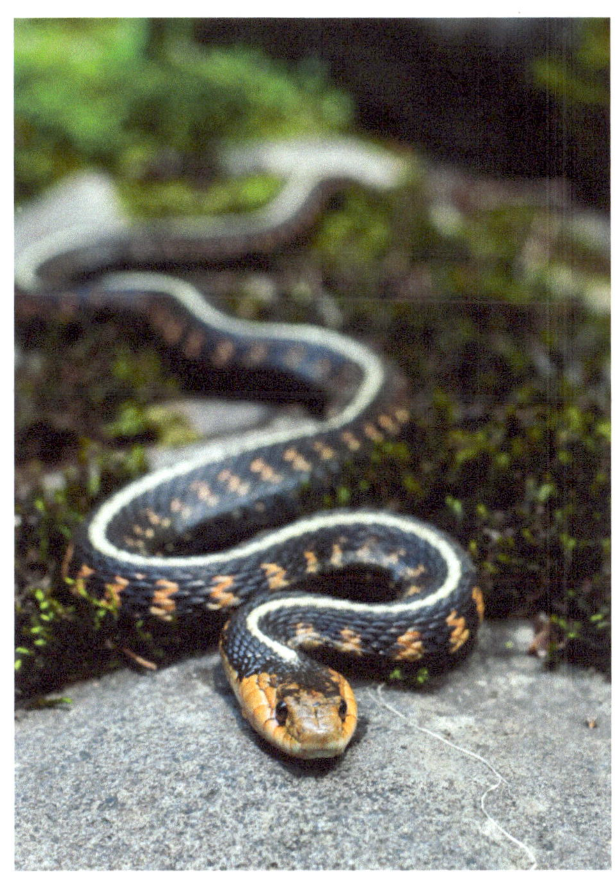

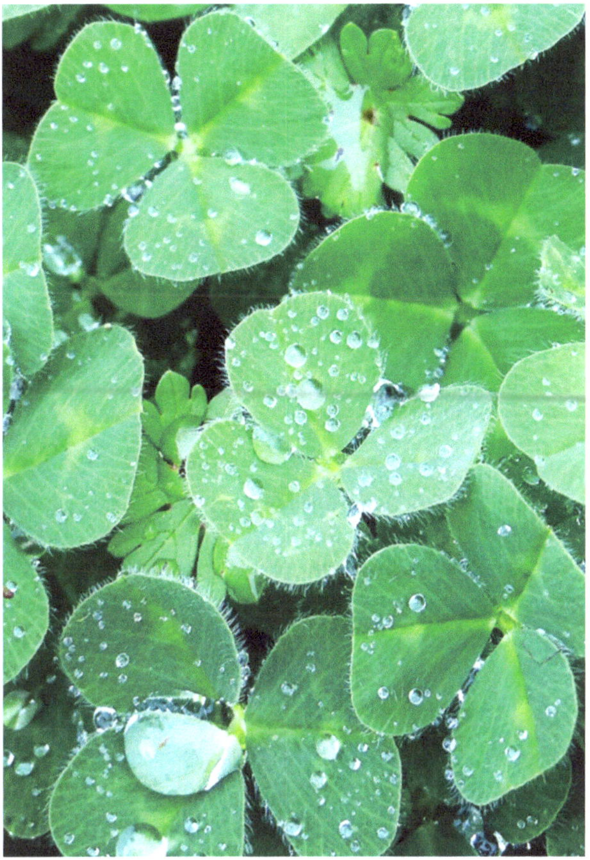

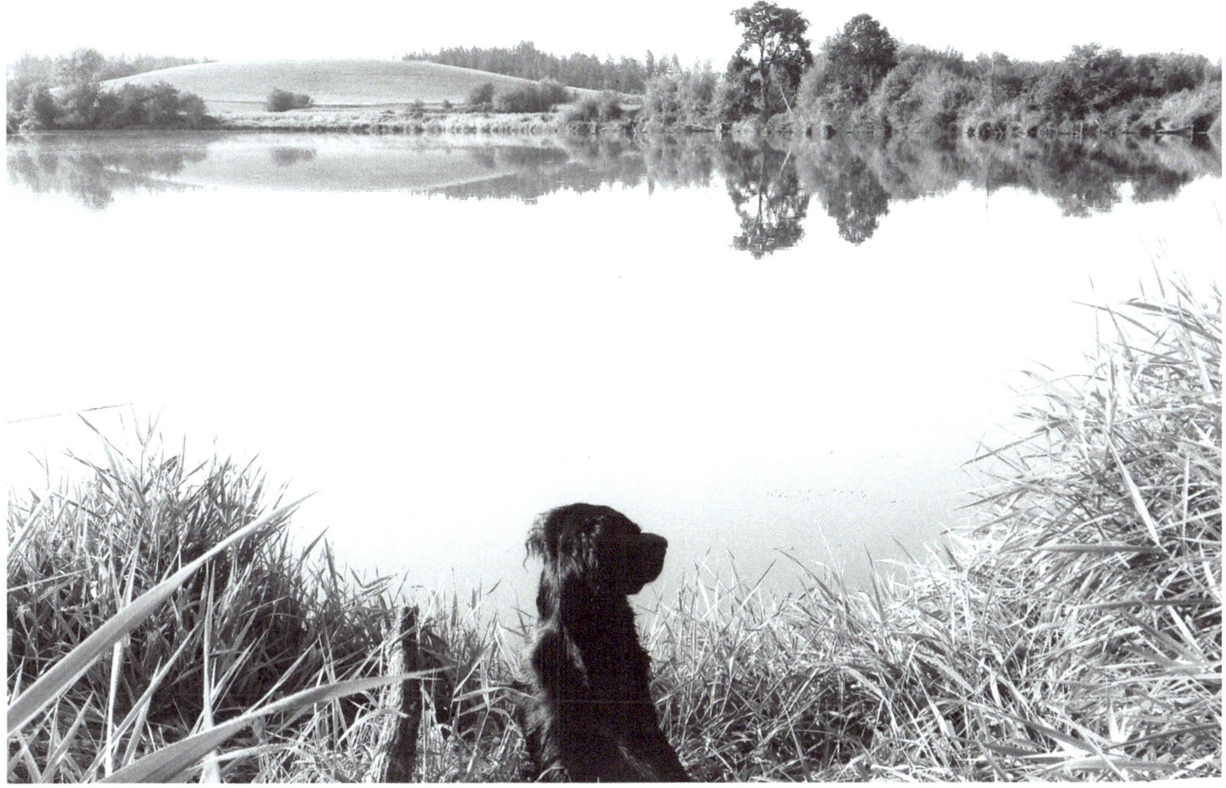

CLAIRE GADBOIS

narrative by Kimberly Su
photographs by Michelle Brown

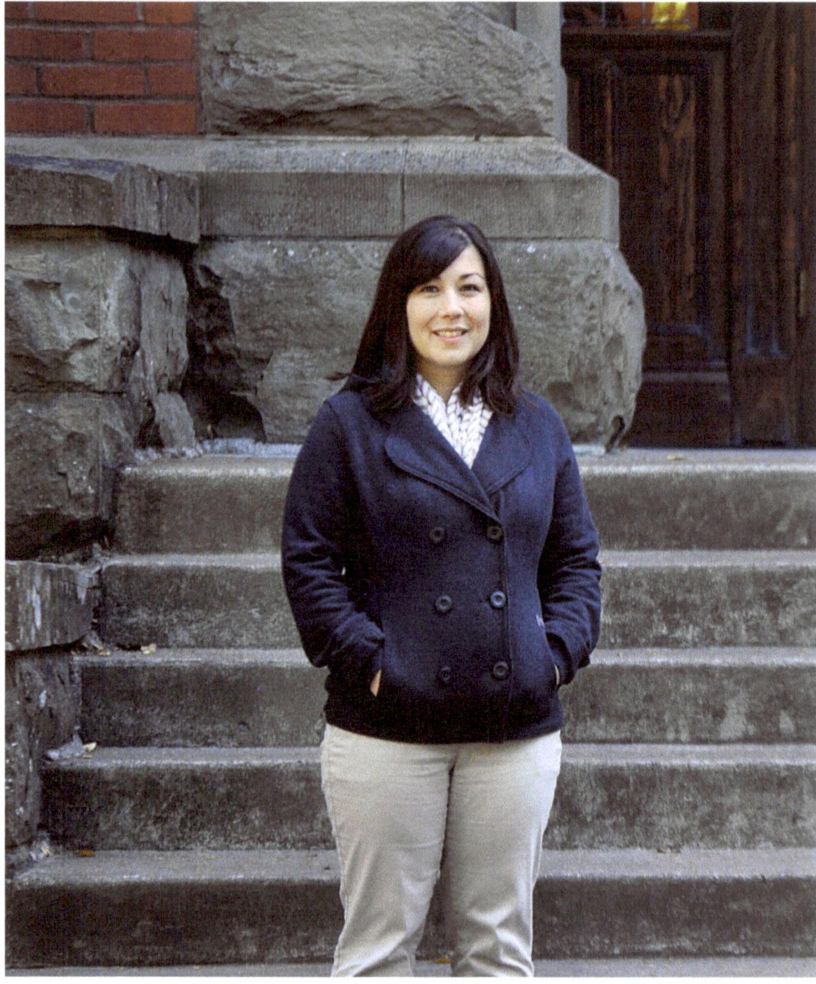

Claire Gadbois works as the liaison between the Registrar and other offices on campus, is in charge of implementing electronic programs and systems that the office uses, and heads the credit certification for student athletes. Her official title is Associate Registrar at Pacific. It's easy to see how busy she can get depending on the time of year. Claire loves her job even though it can be challenging. With a smile in her eyes and a fond voice she says, "When I was first starting out I had a lot of student contact which I really loved and I miss that being in this role. I don't get to interact with students nearly as much as I did before. But I feel like the behind the scenes work I do is important to help students even if they don't realize it."

Claire has been the Associate Registrar at Pacific since 2008. Originally from northern Idaho, Claire graduated from Pacific University in 2003. After her time as a student, she worked in the Registrar's office while an employee was on leave. That was the beginning of Claire's work at Pacific. She started out managing the front desk of the office before switching to the Financial Aid office for a year and a half. After that she returned to be the Assistant Registrar for a few years before her current role.

It's clear that family is important to Claire and while it's obvious from the photos on her desk of her husband, Greg, and their young daughter, Eleanor, her love of family is even more obvious when you walk into her home. When you first step into her house, on the railing of the stairs right by the front door, are photos and colorful drawings done by her daughter. Shoes spill over the rack in the corner; bright colorful tiny shoes, sensible flats and tennis shoes sat together. Claire bends down to put away some plastic blocks to clear the floor and sits on the beige carpet with her daughter following. As Claire talks the one and a half year old Eleanor, plays with some toys, pouting at everyone in the room including her mother. "She's normally pretty talkative, but she's shy with strangers."

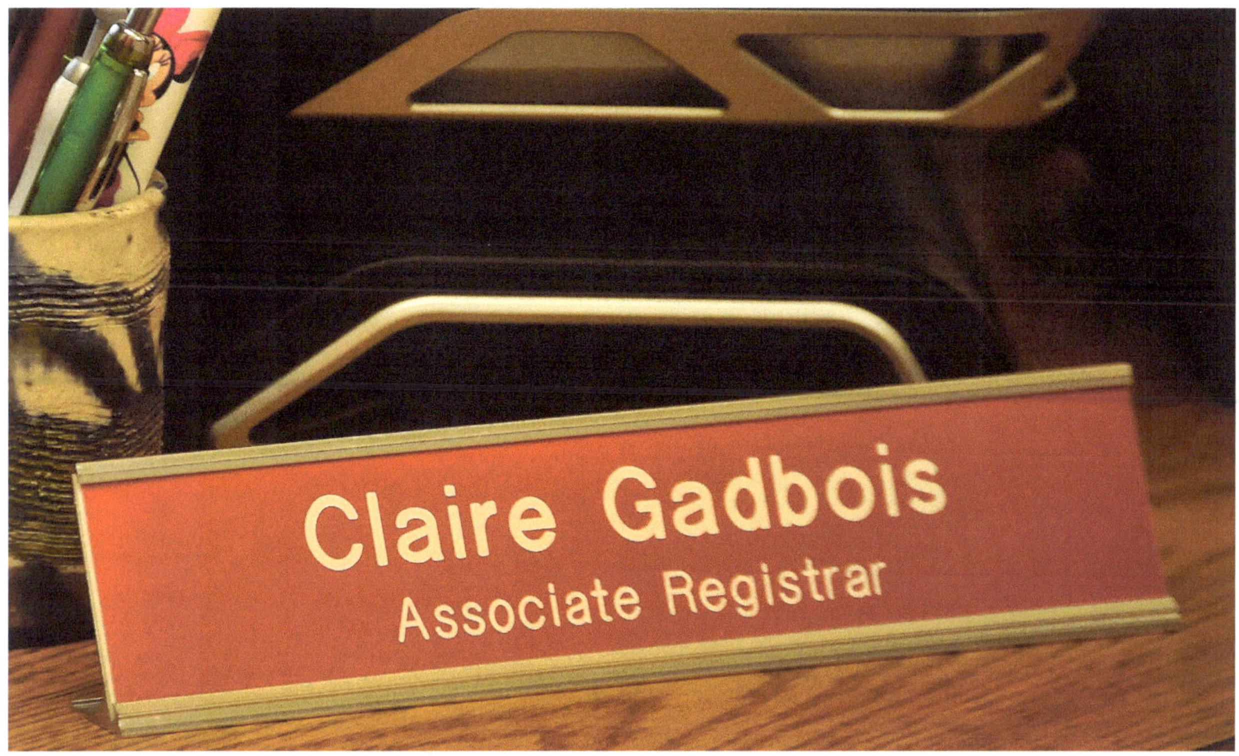

Around the living room, there are framed photos of family on the mantel of the fireplace. Included are a few from her wedding day. Others are photos of nieces and nephews sent by in-laws living in Sioux Falls, South Dakota as well as photos of her only brother's daughters, who live in the Portland metro area. On the wall just above the wooden dining table is a large photo print of a summery scene of Italy that was taken and gifted by family friend, Jim Flory.

"Jim took that when he and his wife were in Italy scouting for a trip." When asked Claire mentions that her and her husband are close with the Florys and that Jim had bought a toy camera for Eleanor. On the wall between the TV and the other side of the dining table on is a large wooden clock. It used to belong to her grandmother, but when her grandmother passed away a few years ago, the clock ended up back with her parents and then fell to her. It's clear that Claire was close to her grandmother, as her daughter is named after her.

"She was really special to me and really to all my cousins. She was just a really special lady, so we decided to [name Eleanor]. I was okay with a middle name but my husband was like no let's do the first name. So I said okay." Claire also points out a framed photograph of a farmhouse and recalls with some nostalgia about how it's a gift from her grandmother of her grandparents' farm in Idaho. Above the couch are some black and white nature prints of Mt. Hood that were taken by a friend of Claire's husband. Right next to those are five large colorful glass ornaments hanging off hooks on the wall that Claire and her husband had blown in a guided class they took in Lincoln City.

Up the stairs to the second floor is the large box filled with a thousand origami cranes, many hung up in the stairwell. Claire, whose family are originally Okinawan Japanese, helped her fold them for her wedding as a tradition of good luck and she has kept them ever since. Another item of note is the large mounted deer head, a

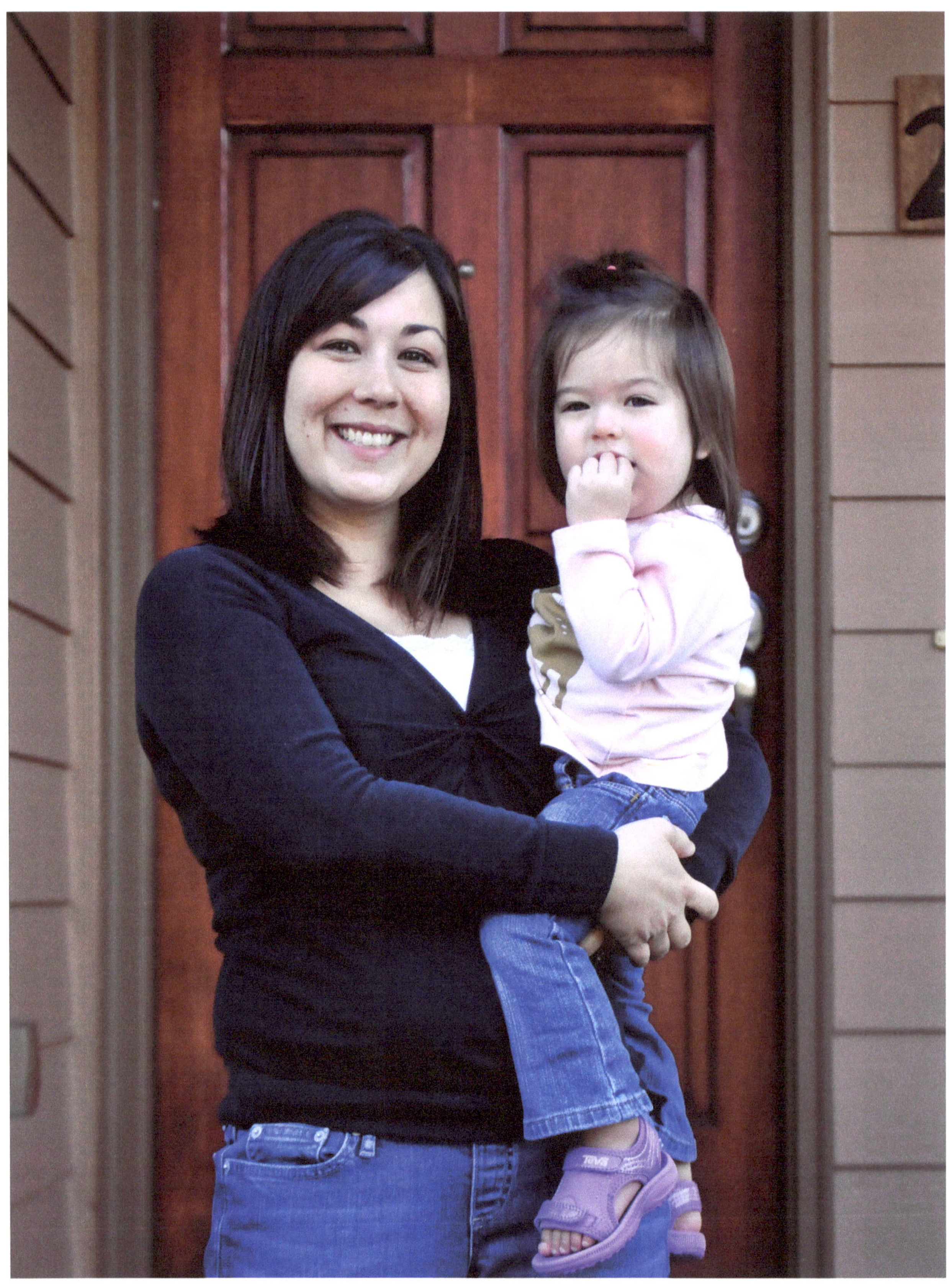

Claire Gadbois | *The People Behind the Scenes of Pacific University*

treasure of her husband who is an avid hunter. He is also interested in woodworking and made the box that holds all those delicate colorful cranes. Claire points at a frame on the wall, "I don't know if you know who Ingrid Unterseher is. She does crossstitch. She did that for us when we got married. She also did this one when Eleanor was born." The pieces are relatively simple decorative flourishes on a white background of fabric. The first which has the couple's names and their wedding date hangs by the stairwell while the other, decorated with Eleanor's name, hangs in their daughter's bedroom.

Claire met her husband off campus at the local Farmer's market through a mutual friend even though both worked at Pacific (Greg was in charge of catering for Aramark). After sharing wine with their mutual friend and a long conversation where she converted him to huckleberries over blueberries, they started dating. They've been married now four years and have another baby due in March. The cozy warm home is hopefully going to be traded in for a large one to make for more space for the new addition to the family when they arrive.

Even though her family is expanding and they have plans to move to the Hillsboro area, Claire is still dedicated to her work at Pacific. She loves her work with students and enjoys the challenging puzzles that arise. Part of her job is to "make sure that all of our student athletes are meeting the academic requirements by the NCAA." Even if it's something like answering the many data requests from academic departments about students, or sending a monthly report to the National Student Clearinghouse so that they can tell the Federal government about Pacific's enrollment statistics, or even things as ordinary as answering questions and emails about policies, Claire is poised. "It's a lot of what I do and it takes up a lot of time," she says, but it's clear from her bright tone that even after nearly ten years, she's not remotely close to closing this chapter of her life.

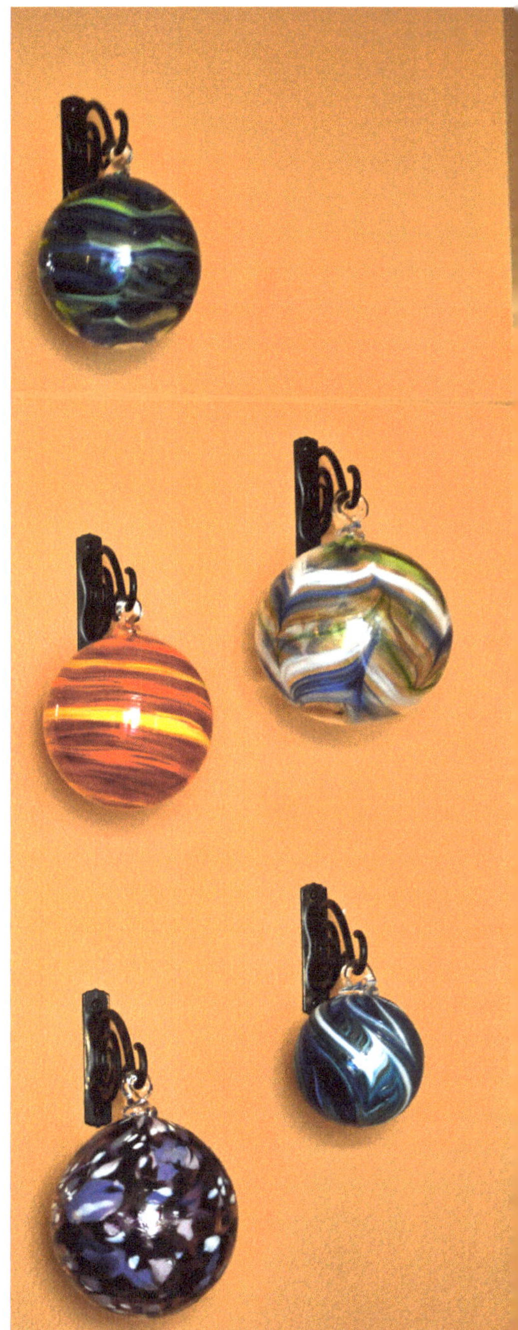

KATIE LARDY

narrative by Shelby Cokeley
photographs by Cody Burkhart

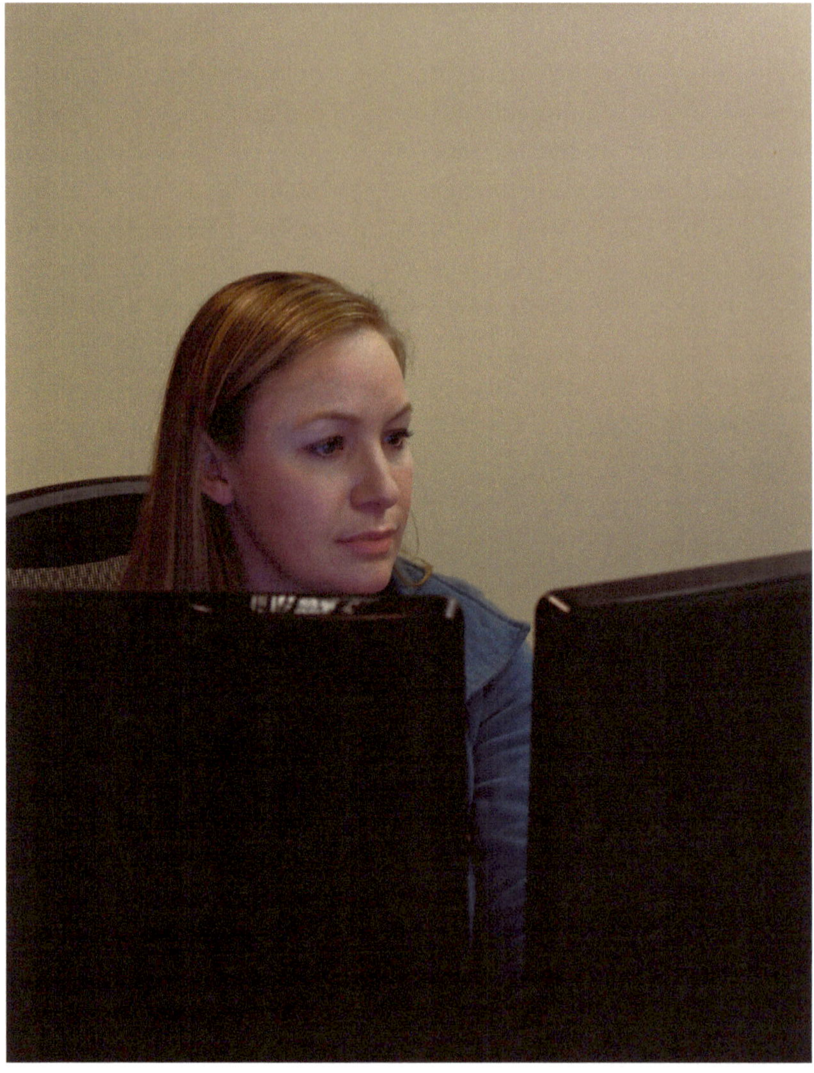

A SERIES OF EMAILS IS SOMETIMES all students ever hear from administration, staff, and professors—another address ending in @pacificu.edu and a serious headshot donning a computer screen. This is what I expected to find when contacting Katie Lardy, Student Services Manager for the School of Communication Sciences & Disorders. However, I was met with something different entirely: warmth.

After a couple mix-ups, a series of messages back and forth, and almost getting lost in the maze that is Berglund hall, Katie opened the door to room 230 with a bright smile on her face and an energy that immediately animated the air. Anyone could tell that Pacific is basically Katie's second home as she sat down comfortably. She has, after all, spent almost two decades with the school in some capacity.

Katie started out as just another student here on campus, graduating in 2003 with a Bachelor of Arts degree in both integrated media and Spanish. "I didn't always have plans to come back to Pacific. I don't think any of this was scripted, it's just the path life naturally followed," Katie says about her return to campus in a new capacity.

After graduation Katie spent three years working for Intel, serving as a Marketing Coordinator for the company's Intel Teach to the Future Program. "I played that sort of connecting role, helping teachers implement new technology into their classroom strategy through the company," she says recalling the time she spent with the large corporate entity.

The dubious look on my face must have said it all, "I know it seems like quite the contrast working for such a large company and now being in such an intimate setting like Pacific," she says in response. "I really appreciate all of my past work experience, though. Intel really allowed me to learn and experience the corporate

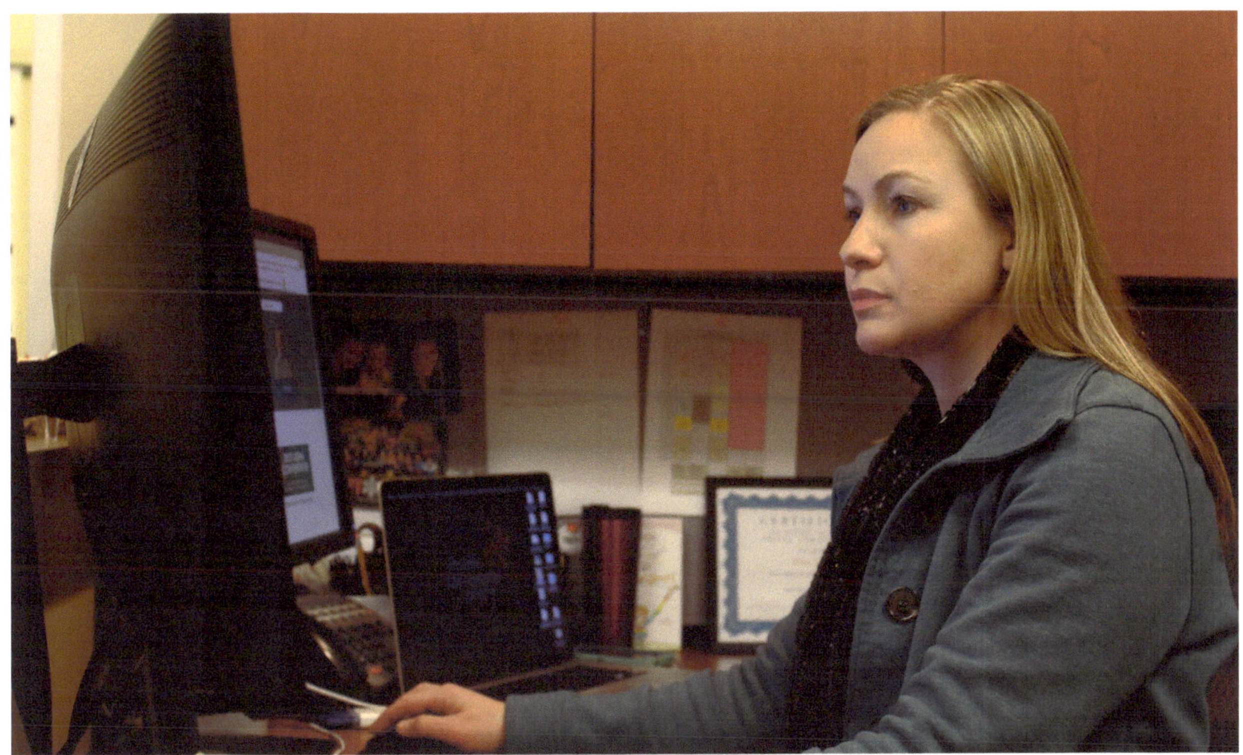

work ethic," this she says is something that has served her well in the both of the positions she has held with Pacific.

Spending nine years in the Career Development Center as the Assistant Director and Pathways Coordinator while also coordinating the Advantage Scholars Program, Katie was ready to apply her skills to other areas. Now working alongside pre-health professions Katie is able to help students make the connections they need to and gain experience for their future field. "I have such a respect for their work," Katie expresses while further explaining her gratitude for the dedicated students and faculty she works with on a daily basis.

While her work experience has provided her with innumerable opportunities and a list of skillsets that could rival the best, the most beneficial lessons Katie has learned come from a less professional place. It was here at Pacific where her core belief and skill of treating others with respect and understanding, "Treating humans as humans," as she puts it, was reinforced as an undergraduate.

This idea of warmth and overall understanding of others is something Katie carries far beyond her desk at Pacific. Her two young daughters Bella and Bailey have been influenced through this same mentality. Katie laughs as I ask about potential hobbies or activities that she indulges in to wind

down from such a demanding job, "Hobbies? My kids are my hobbies!" Though she admits her love for salsa dancing (discovered while on a study abroad trip via Pacific to Ecuador), Katie says life is more about enjoying precious time with her family these days.

"I'm always grateful for that little bit of time I can spend with my girls," she says smiling. "Work can be demanding and I may not be able to everything I want to, like missing volunteer opportunities that happen during my work day, but I make it work and find that balance." Being a full-time working mother of two has its challenges but that does not stop Katie from thriving in the workplace and playing an active role in

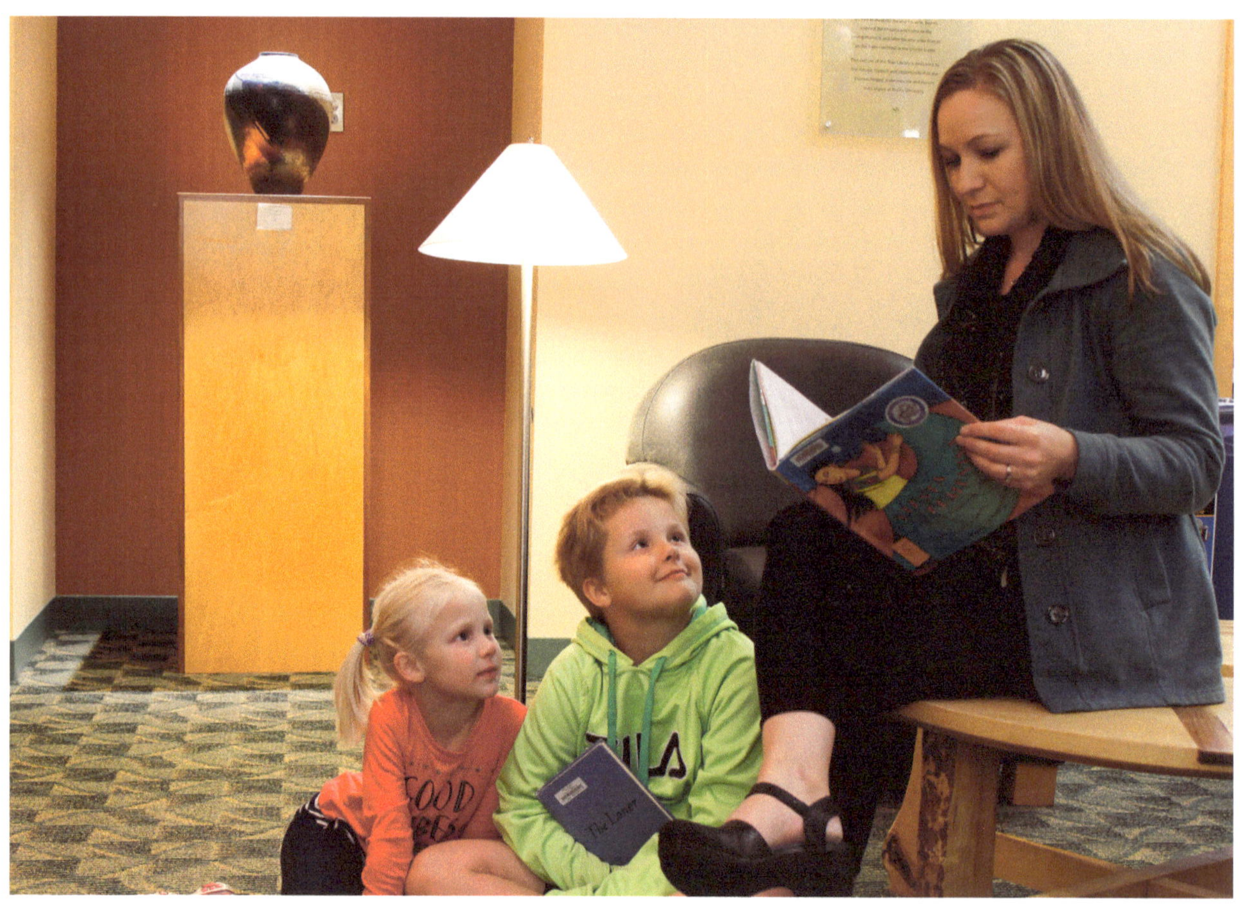

her children's lives—like being the "Small Ball Rep" on her daughter's basketball team or reading bedtime stories every night.

Although I think she may disagree with me, it seems like Katie really does do everything.

"Work can be demanding and I may not be able to everything I want to…but I make it work and find that balance."

Just as our meeting was coming to a close, both sides of Katie—the loving mother and successful Pacific staff member—combined so clearly and bubbled to the surface one last time. Selflessly she asks about my studies, connected to media just as hers were during her time at Pacific, and offers me information and contacts she thinks I may be interested in. I am. I am also grateful.

Before I know it, another student is asking for Katie's assistance, "Oh, I didn't mean to interrupt, I can have so-and-so help me if you're busy!" the young woman says. "No, no, no, I'll be right there, it's no problem!" Katie says coolly, jumping up from her chair, she is already off to provide her abundance of work and personal skills to someone else.

So maybe life is not always salsa dancing in foreign countries for Katie. Maybe sometimes it is hectic days at work, providing her unique skillset to the benefit of others. Maybe sometimes it is the peaceful nights spent at home reading bedtime stories to her kids. For Katie Lardy it is all about finding a balance.

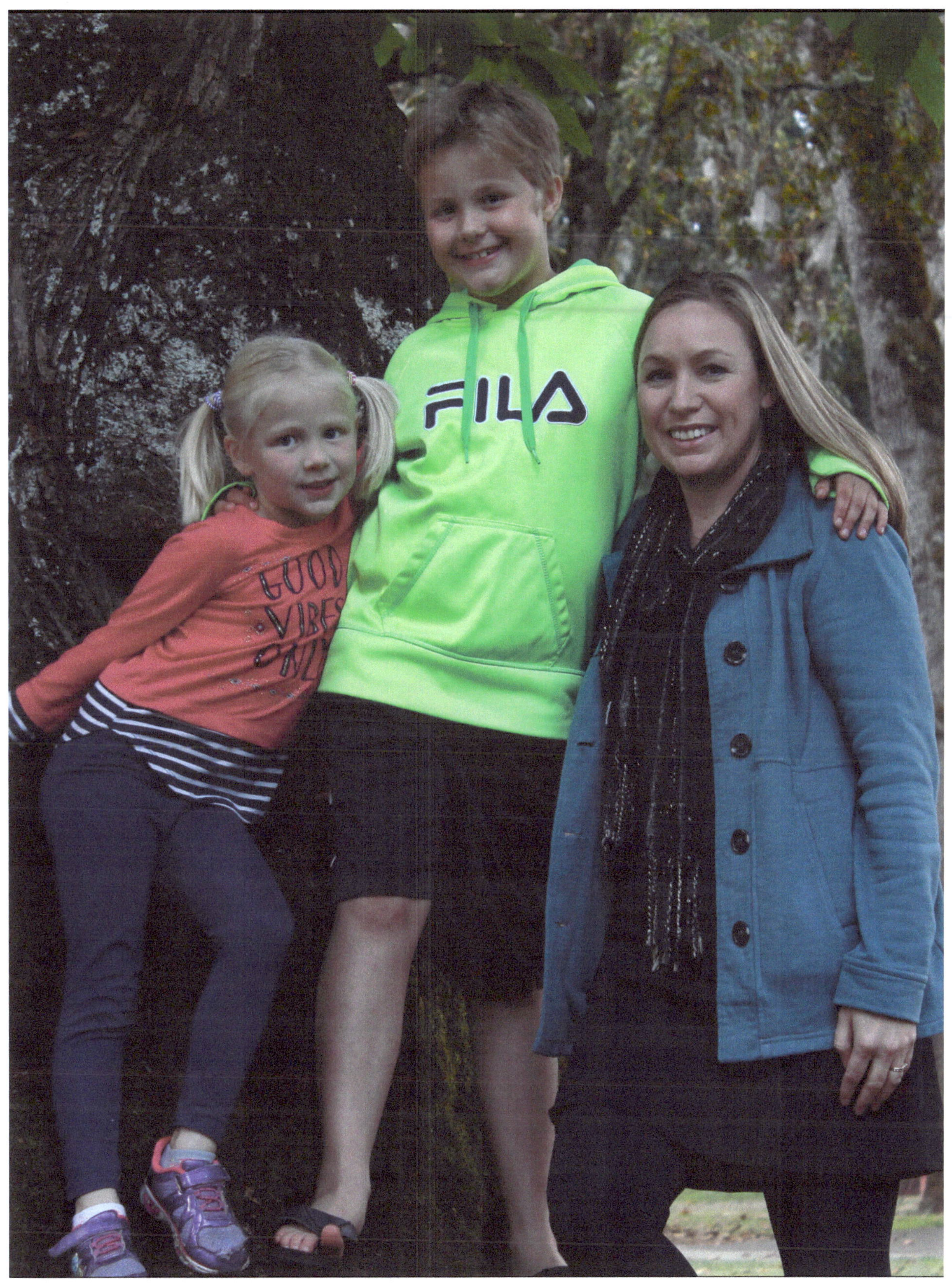

FILA
GOOD VIBES ONLY

SAM MORRISON

narrative by Angel Martinez Rosas
photographs by La'imana Grace

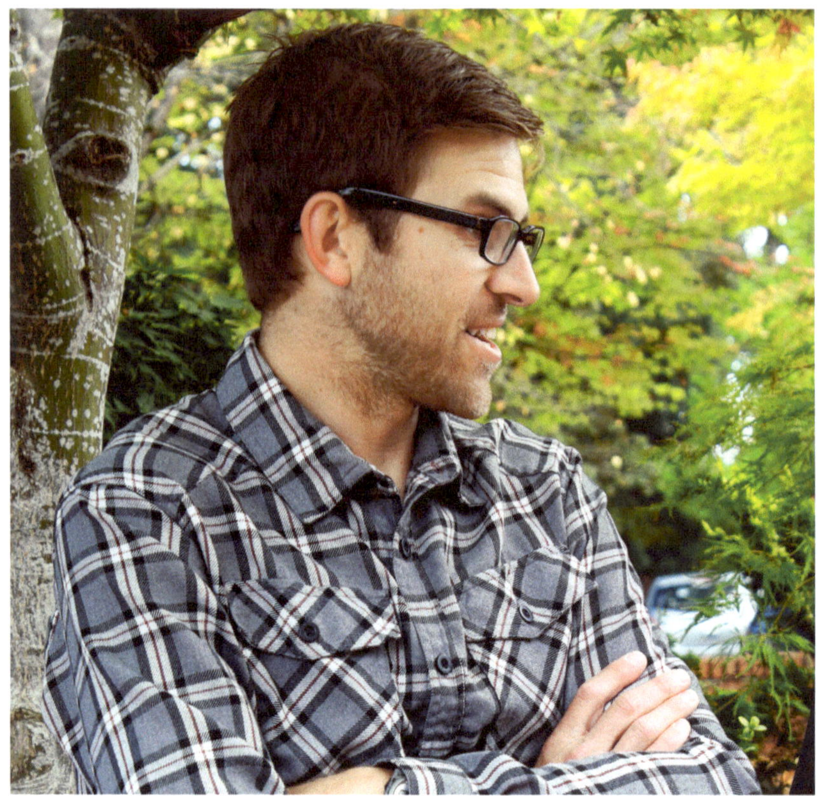

AFTER ORDERING A TWO-DOLLAR-and-fifty-cent breakfast at McDonald's, Sam Morrison turns to me and says, "You should also write that I'm thrifty." He has deemed his quotidian routine as Assistant Director of Outdoor Pursuits too unremarkable for me to observe and has instead invited me on a whitewater rafting trip to the Clackamas River. We are joined by three of his students who are training to become paddle guides in rafting. He dons a red raincoat, contact lenses, and an impish grin, a contrast from the bespectacled professor, resplendent in faded plaid I had met earlier in the week. "Are you ready?" he asks with unrestrained enthusiasm.

This enthusiasm for the outdoors was begotten by a "formative experience" he had when he was eighteen years old and pulled over to the side of a dirt road in Mexico to eat at a taco stand. He fondly recalls sitting in his car with his friend, devouring lengua tacos he ordered in clumsy Spanish. "I grew up in a small town from Colorado, so my concept of travel was that you had to have quite a bit of money—you have to buy a package, essentially, like a cruise or a resort vacation or a big hotel. You couldn't just go down and drive across the border and kind of figure it out." At the time, Sam held no desire to travel. "It was something rich people did. That's why the tacos were so formative. It was the experience of eating and interacting [with the locals], being around people and civilization. It showed me that you can just buy a one-way ticket for yourself to anywhere."

Which is what Sam promptly did. He took a break from his studies as a Studio Art major at Colorado Mesa University and bought a ticket to Nairobi, Kenya. An impulse fostered a habit, and he would eventually earn his bachelor of science in environmental science in 2010 after six years of studies fractured by frequent travels. Throughout those six years and those that followed, he has travelled to thirty-five countries, including Argentina, Chile, Uruguay, Peru, Colombia, Panama, and Costa Rica. It becomes increasingly apparent, however, that his favorite country is Mexico. He became so enamored that he was compelled to move there where he resided comfortably for four years. He bashfully admits to frequenting salsa clubs "at least twice a month" during the three years he spent in Guadalajara.

As we continue our drive towards the river, Sam discusses how he attained Spanish fluency with the

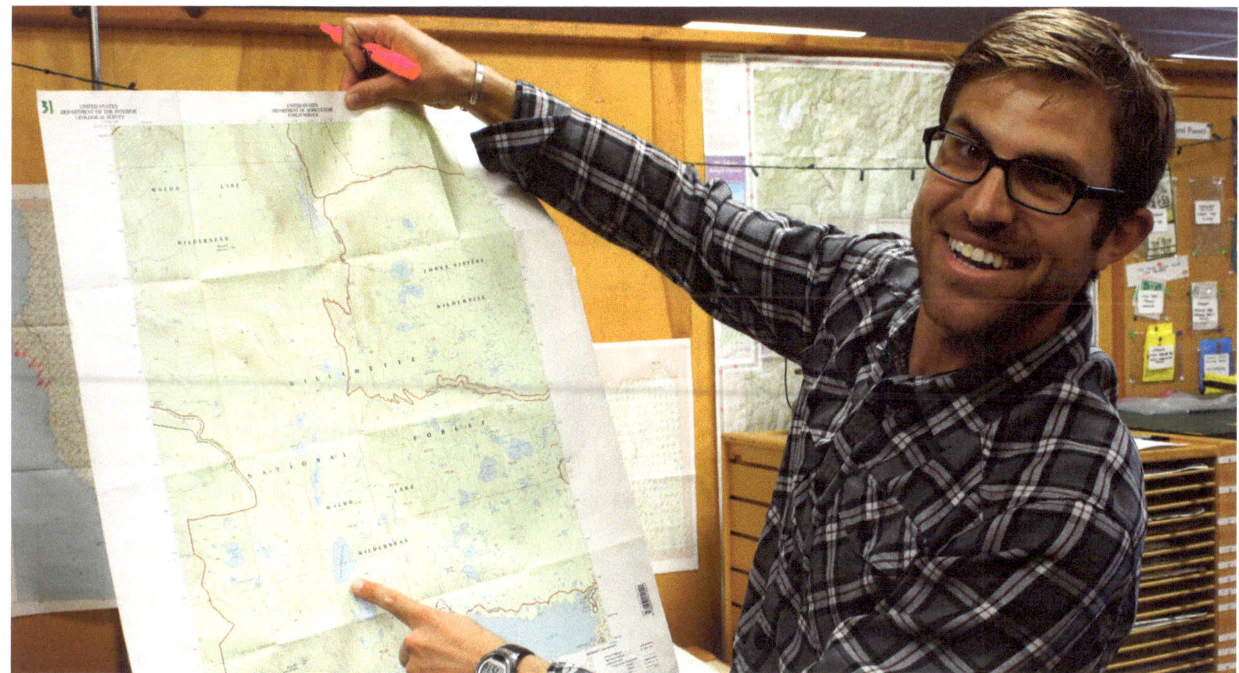

aid of his girlfriends in Mexico. One student gently mocks with a sibilant "Girlfriendsss?" Sam becomes flustered. "How about you write girlfriend?" he asks me. It is amusing to observe Sam and his students fall into an easy rapport. His previous comment in McDonald's about being "thrifty" earned laughter and garnered a few jabs at his frugal tendencies. Sam rejects the label of "cheap," however, and insists on "thrifty." He informs me that he is merely saving money for new gear and equipment; his students do not think it justifies his unabashed affinity for Little Caesar's pizza.

We arrive at the river and prepare the raft. Brisk air gnaws at our noses and grey clouds threaten to encroach, but good humor prevails. Someone comments that Sam's new drysuit makes him look like Buzz

Lightyear. Sam laughs. Once on the water, they become synchronized as students rotate the role of paddle guide and navigate rapids of varying classes (or 'difficulty'). He praises one who successfully avoids a large rock and encourages another as we approach a rapid they dub "the toilet bowl." It is obvious that a profound camaraderie exists between those in Outdoor Pursuits, one they acknowledge is nurtured by the solitude of the wilderness and bolstered by defecating in the woods under compulsion. "Having no bathroom really brings us together," one student comments.

Sam became aware of a position available at Pacific University's outdoor program two years ago while he was still living in Mexico— southern Baja California—browsing online ads. I note it requires more

effort to prod Sam into discussing the aspects of his job that take place in the office. "I spend a couple hours a day doing lesson planning, a little bit of grading. Right now, I teach Intro to Outdoor Leadership, Intro to Kayaking, and Intro to Expedition Planning. I plan a lot of recreational trips for students." He adds, "I answer about fifty emails per day." I ask if there was ever a terrifying moment during an Outdoor Pursuits trip. Without hesitation, he says, "There are no terrifying moments in Outdoor Pursuits."

In addition to admiring the state's beauty and being beguiled by ample sites ready for exploration, a specific passion of his also drew him to Oregon: "Hood River up north is kayaking central. People come from all over to kayak in the Columbia River Gorge. Nobody is interested,

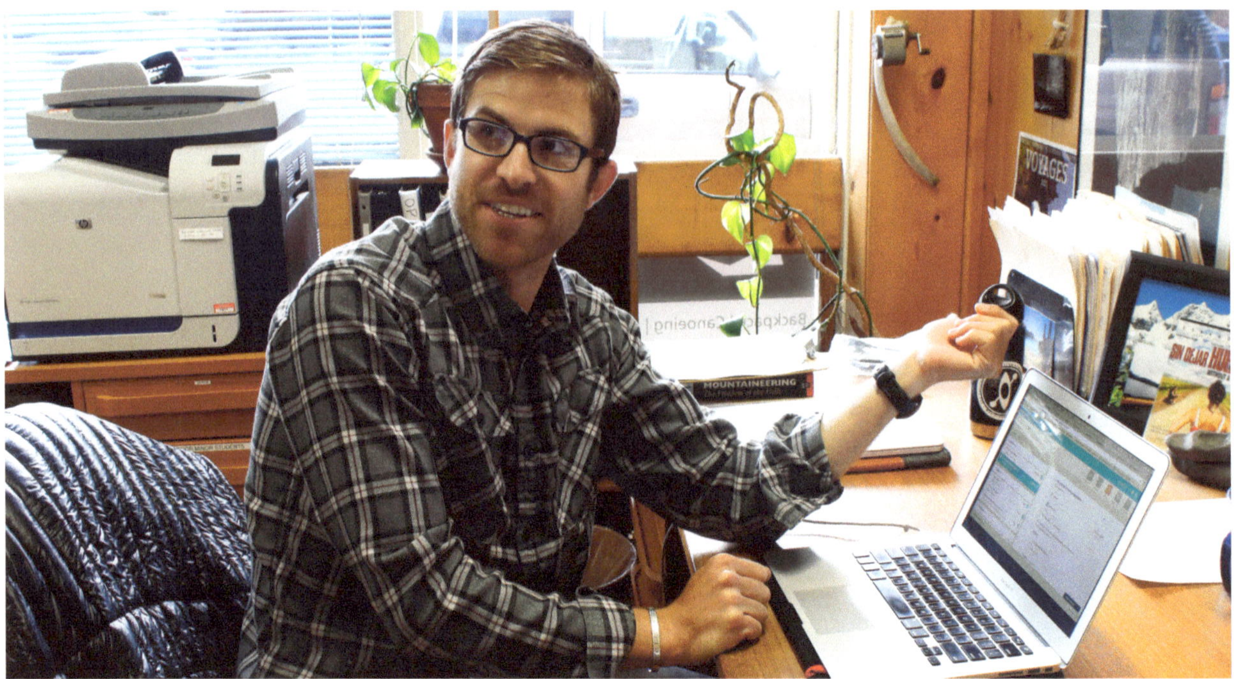

though. We have this saying: 'You know you're a kayaker when nobody cares.'" He shrugs that off with a laugh. His role at Pacific University seems molded specifically for him, and he expresses pleasure in having found a way to mix his career with his passion. Returning to a university setting is fitting for him, as it was the outdoor program at Colorado Mesa University—the same program that led him to that taco stand in Mexico—that awoke his insatiable desire to travel. "It changed my life, transformed it. More than my degree."

As our raft glides through the river, a large bird flies overhead. "That's an osprey!" Sam points and informs us that ospreys feed exclusively on fish and possess special characteris-tics that allow them to dive directly into water to catch its prey. "They're my favorite bird of prey." A jest is tossed at Sam's expense for naming a favorite bird of prey. "You can't just have one favorite bird," Sam retorts.

After I ask about other activities he enjoys, he answers with "climbing" and reveals an impressive list of peaks he has climbed: Mt. Kilimanjaro in 2006; Aconcagua, the tallest peak in South America, in 2009; and Denali in 2011. "At least, those are the ones I put on my résumé." He thinks for a moment after being asked which peak he would like to climb one day. "I like a challenge.… I think I would like to climb a Himalayan peak." After a beat: "Not Everest, though. Everyone climbs Everest, you know? It's too cliché."

The Clackamas River has been successfully navigated and the crew, some more sodden than others, lift their paddles in the air and crash them together in a celebratory "paddle five." A light rain begins while my questions devolve into frivolity. Sam and I discover our birthdays are a day apart, and we agree that we both enjoy the company of a fellow Sagittarius. Some time later he makes an offhand comment: "I've dated a lot of Pisces." Sam congratulates his students on their work and arranges for them to congregate at a Little Caesar's in Portland for a meal. Once we are in the warmth of the school van, Sam turns the radio to NPR; his students groan.

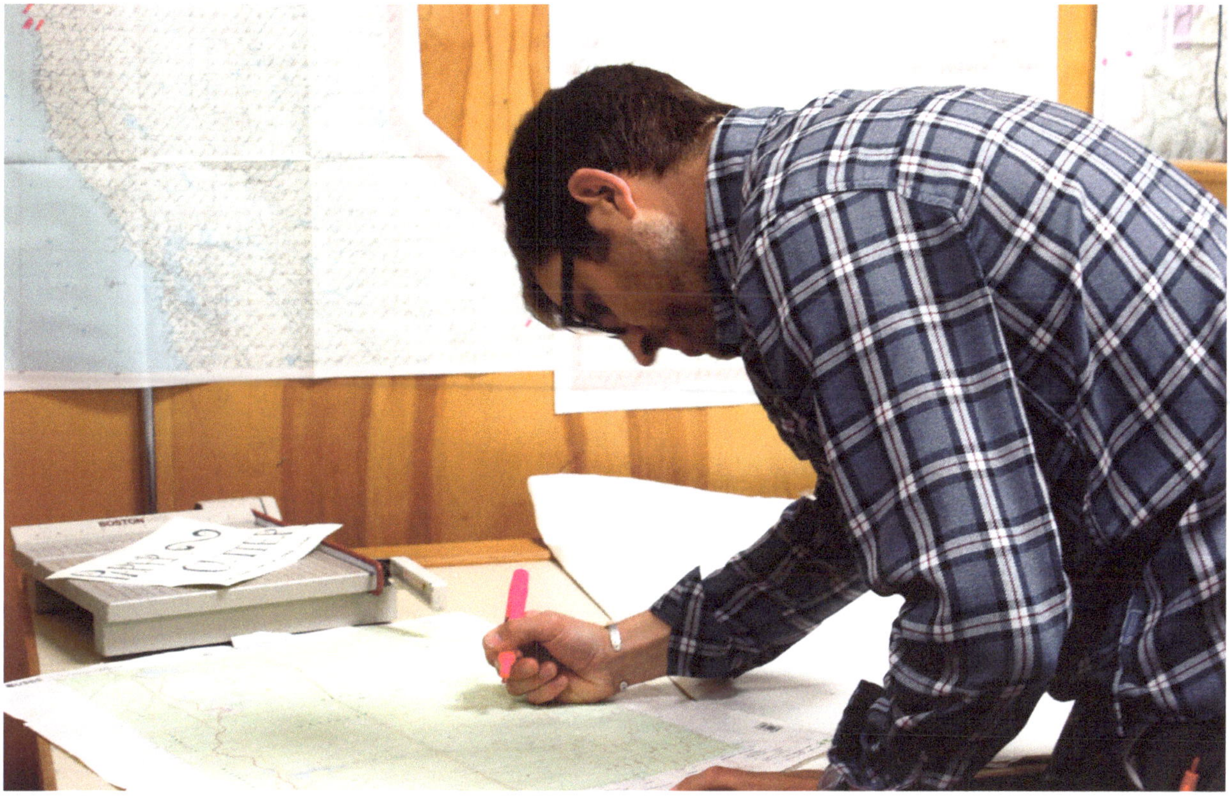

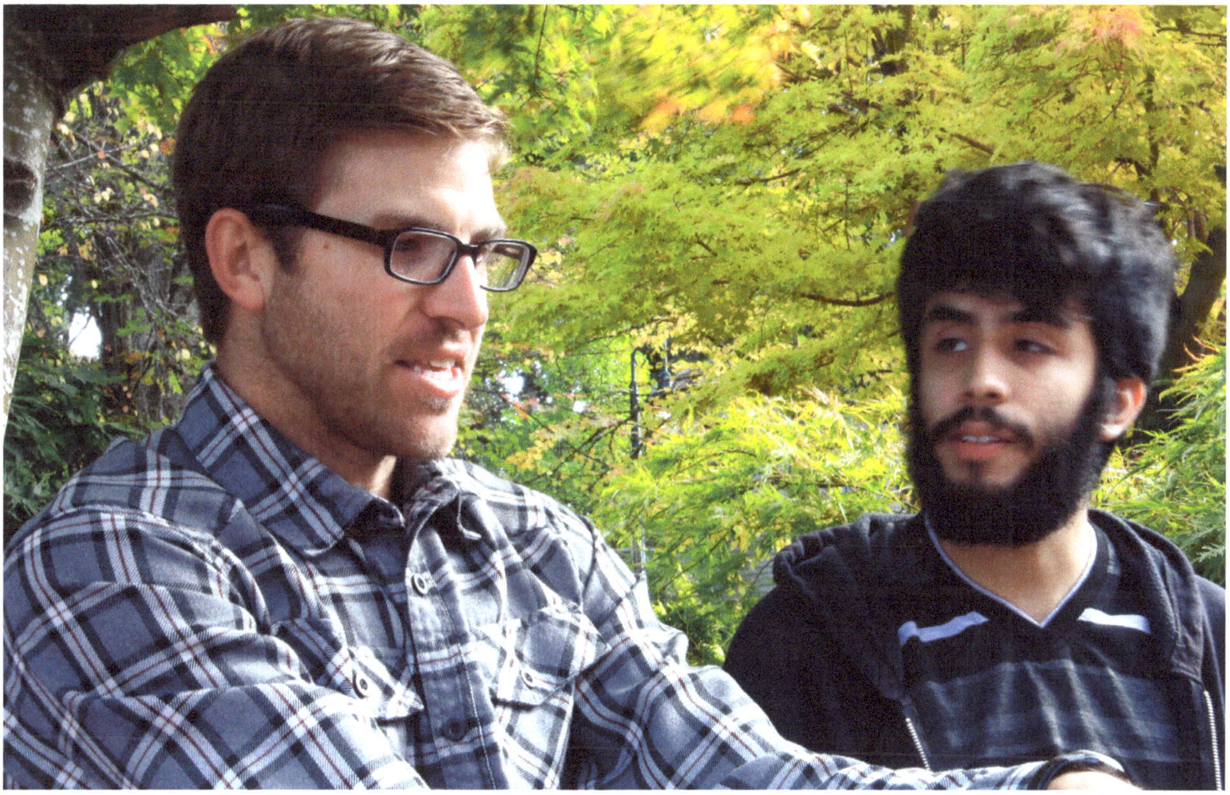

BRIAN O'DRISCOLL

narrative by Rachel Savini
photographs by Tanner Boyle

SOMETIMES LIFE IS ALL ABOUT connections, and no one takes this more to heart than Brian O'Driscoll. Brian is the Director of the Career Center at Pacific University. His main focus is helping students answer the "what's next" question that comes after graduation. Pacific pride runs strong in his family. He, his father, and his siblings all attended Pacific, and he has high hopes for his oldest son to attend next fall. He graduated Pacific as a Literature and Philosophy major, so how did he find his way to Chapman Hall? Brian O'Driscoll wanted to do meaningful work and to help himself and others validate their Liberal Arts Education. He interacts with alumni on a daily basis to connect students with graduates working in the professional world, it's one of his favorite parts of the job. "It's a great joy to have students who have gone on to graduate and still be able to rekindle a conversation with them," he says.

What you might not know about this soft spoken man in Chapman Hall is that he is a theatre fan, although he insists that he

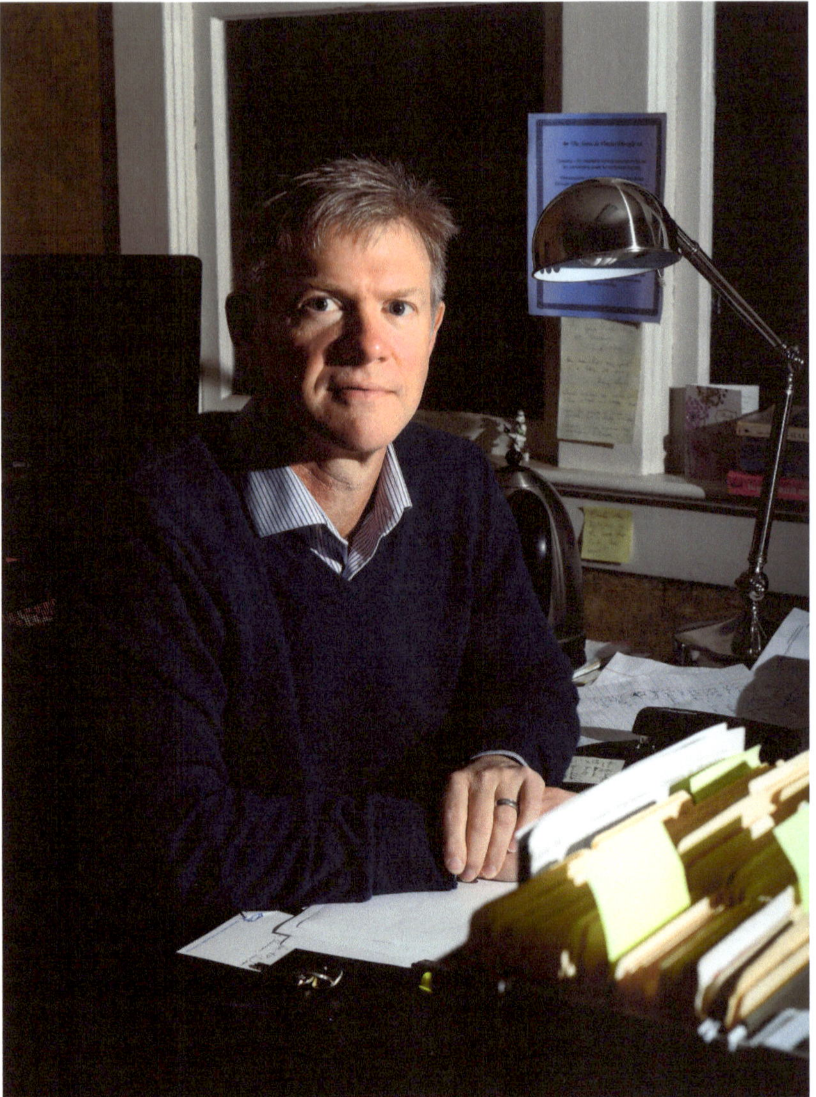

only watches. His favorite place on campus is the Tom Miles Theatre, which he swears hasn't changed since he was a student. Brian says it's "magic to see students acting or dancing and they are so put together and professional." He strives to help students implement that confidence into their upcoming careers.

Outside of campus, you can find Brian running his family's blueberry farm. "The farm is the dog that wags the tail in our lives," he says. Farming is something that runs in the O'Driscoll family. Following in his parents footsteps, he now runs a farm of his own after growing up on one his entire life. It's easy to see that Brian has a real passion for farming. His eyes light up as he tells me the ins and outs of blueberry season, chuckling when he points out how any birthdays or anniver-

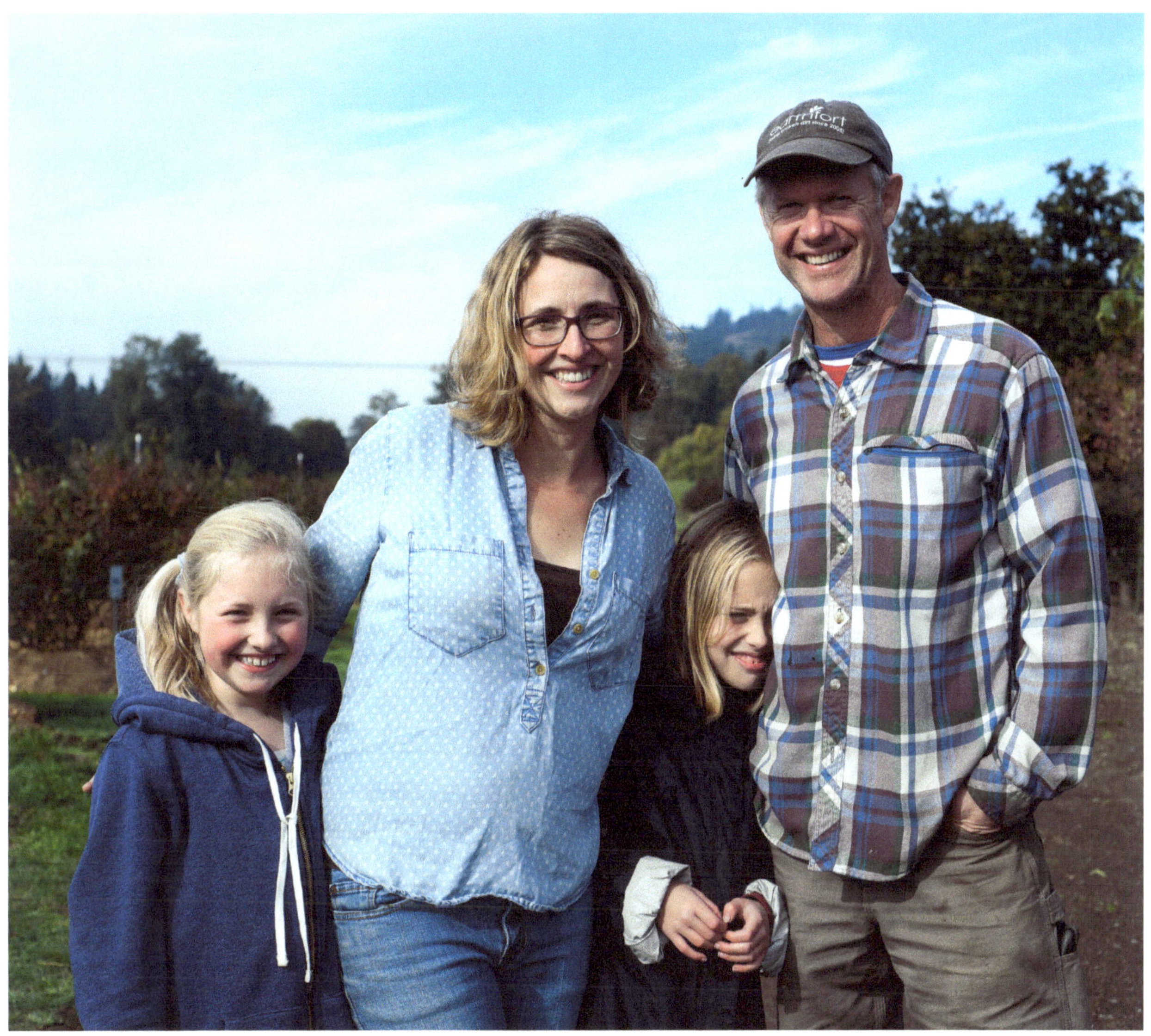

saries that happen during that time are put on the back burner. "My parents gave me the best of what the farm had to offer. I chose to go back to it and it frequently kicks my butt." The farm is another way to create connections within his own community. Brian talks lovingly about showing people around the farm and helping people with all of their berry needs. He's all about helping people find opportuni-

ties, on campus and on the farm. He shakes his head in amusement, and huffs as he tells me about the local high school and middle school students who help on the farm during the year. "There's nothing like knowing you have orders that need to get out the door and on the freeway up to Portland and you're watching kids in the field throwing blueberries at each other."

Brian's work doesn't end with graduation or with blueberry season, not by a longshot. Brian has high hopes for the Career Center in the future to strengthen its bond with Pacific alumni. He possesses a passion for working with alumni, not only to help make connections with the students, but to help them with the next steps in their professional careers. "I have witnessed many alumni who definitely could benefit

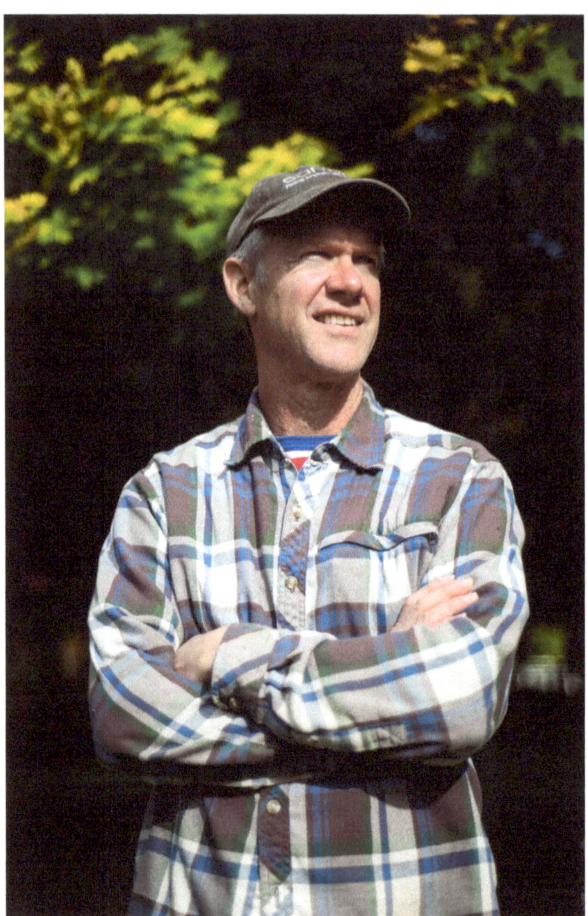
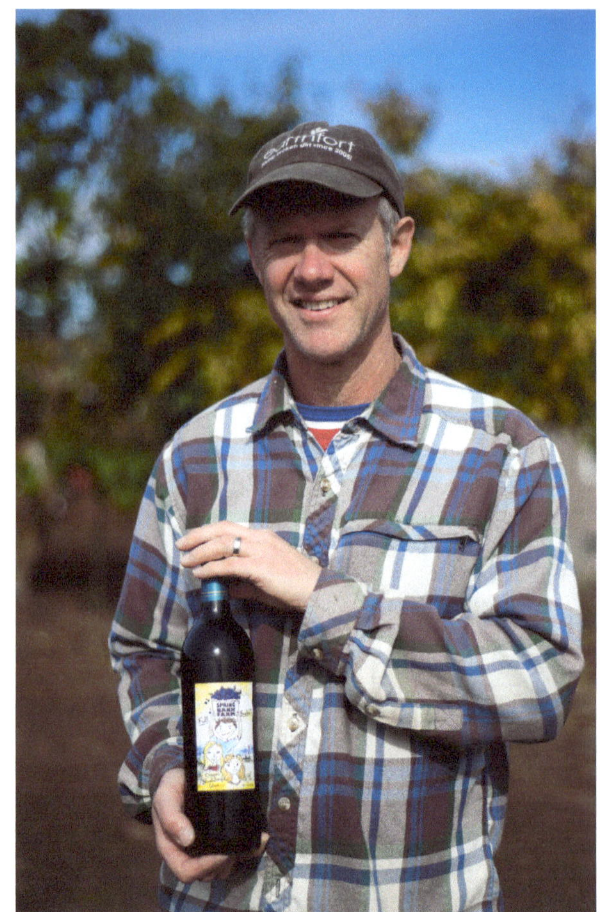

from a little bit of career conversation," he says. Boxer Pride is an important part of Brian O'Driscoll's life, and he wants it to be known that it doesn't stop after graduation. Pacific continues to be a source for guidance, counseling, and just a shoulder to lean on. All you have to do is dial Chapman Hall for an earful of knowledge, and if you're lucky, a handful of blueberries.

"It's a great joy to have students who have gone on to graduate and still be able to rekindle a conversation with them."

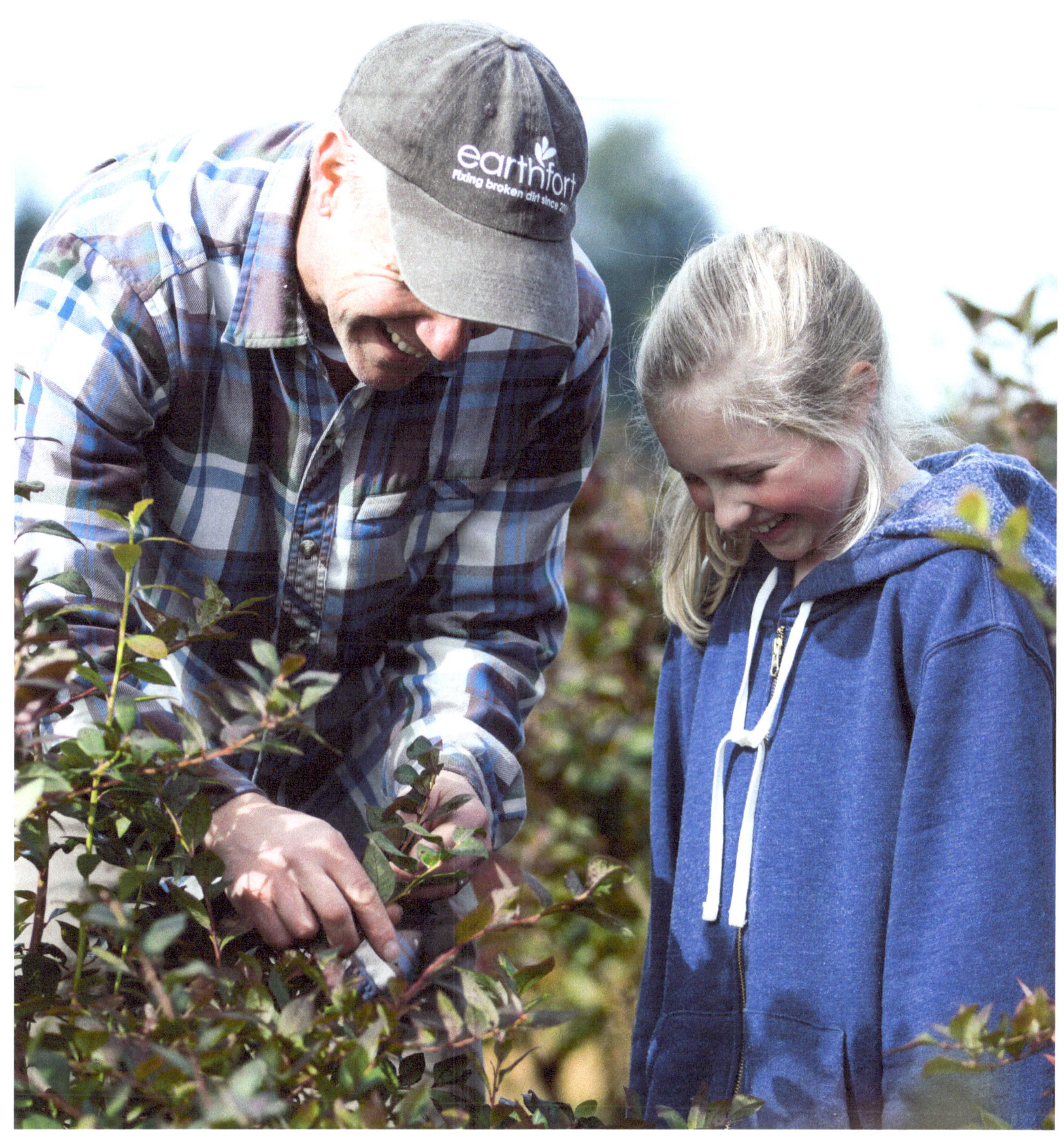

NARCE RODRIGUEZ

Narrative by Sophia Backus
Photographs by Macie Akai

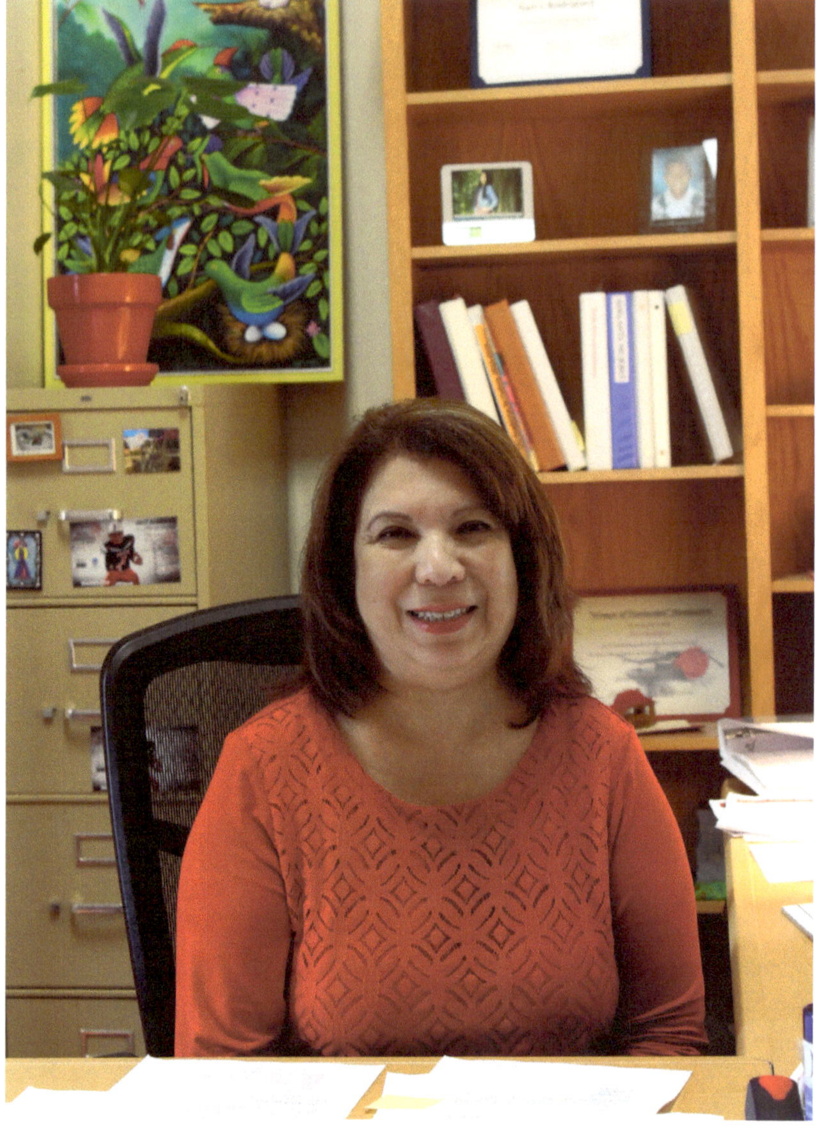

Narce Rodriguez is a difficult woman to find. She's split across all six of Pacific University's campuses, and a trip to the Health Professions location in Hillsboro seemed my only chance to meet this bustling woman.

I walk down hallways lined with lockers and professionals in their twenties and beyond. They are friendly and greet me as I search for the elusive room 211. It's not there. I do another loop and at the end of the hall, I see 211 right in front of me, with three large signs blatantly marking it. Inside the small office, I see Narce on a call. She pauses the conversation to come out and ask for a few more minutes, an apologetic smile on her face. A few minutes later, she waves me into her bare office, phone cord still tying her to her desk. A few salutations and she ends the call. "Sorry about that. That was my old boss at PCC [Portland Community College]. We're working to make a bridge program," she explains, moving aside her computer and folding her hands on her desk. Specifically, they are working with the School of Business to make it easier to transition into Pacific's program from PCC. "Today has been hectic. It's my first day at this location."

While it may be her first day in this office, Narce has been working nonstop at Pacific since July of 2017. Narcedalia Rodriquez, better known as Narce, is the Chief Equity Diversity Inclusion Officer at Pacific University. While she is new to this university, she has worked at many others, including OSU, Arizona State University, Portland State University, and PCC. She started off as a recruitment officer at OSU and eventually became the Dean of Students at PCC.

Throughout the interview, she repeatedly expresses that students

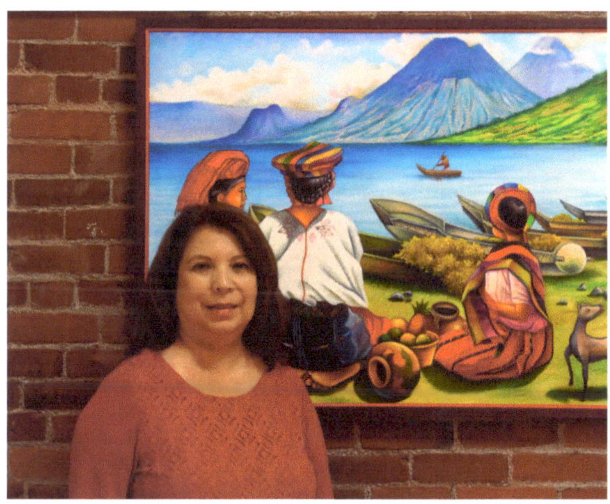 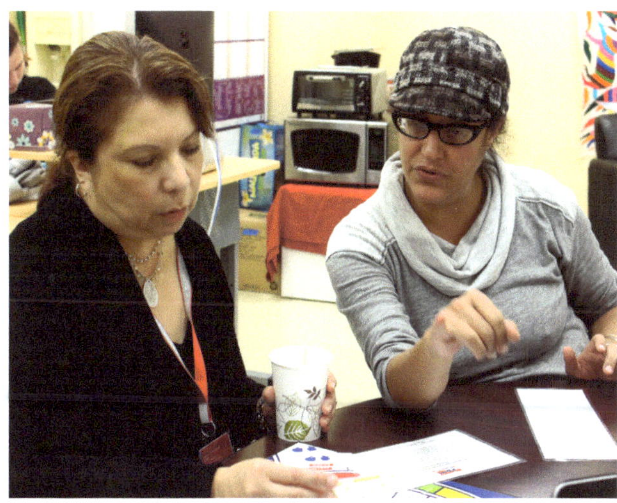

are her favorite part about working at Pacific and other colleges.

"I'm a nerd," she tells me, laughing. "I love school." Narce attended OSU for her undergraduate degrees in Sociology and Spanish and Master's degree in Interdisciplinary Studies, specifically in Class, Race, and Gender as well as Women's Studies. She began her college career at OSU with a one year scholarship available to migrant workers and their children. "They provided us one year of tuition money to kind of get us set up and then the years after that we were sort of on our own, but at least it gave us that foundation to kinda get our feet wet with what college is about." It was enough to get her hooked on higher education and she's enthusiastically continued hers through the years while helping others do the same.

Growing up, she moved from state to state, across the country, as a migrant worker with her family. When she was seven, her parents decided to send her to Mexico for some stability at home and in school. Even when they moved permanently to Oregon in 1976, Mexico still felt like home. When she lived in Oregon, "there were many barriers, like language, and we were one of the few Mexican families in town. So we always felt like the outsiders." At that point in her life, however, it was time for her to go to college. She took time between her Masters and PhD programs to have her two daughters before deciding to continue on. Just a year in, however, events beyond her control prevented her from finishing her PhD program. She chose to leave to have more time for her two daughters, both quite young at the time, and her husband, sick from his time serving in the Gulf War. While she doesn't want to take on the financial burden of the PhD program now, just a hand-ful of years away from retirement, she still takes classes on empowerment and career advancement to scratch that school-loving itch.

Narce has lived in the Cornelius-Forest Grove area for nearly twenty years, but has known and loved the area since her days working at OSU as a recruiter. "I just liked the community and I liked that I could go into a high school and see people that looked like me," she explains. "And I would look forward to coming [here] because I could get some tacos," she adds enthusiastically, dissolving into laughter. Apparently, when she was in school, the closest taquerias to Corvallis were either in Woodburn or Forest Grove. She adds, "there's a lot of work that needs to be done, but I feel very welcome."

At Pacific University, she's been working tirelessly to get the Multicultural Center, a new student-led

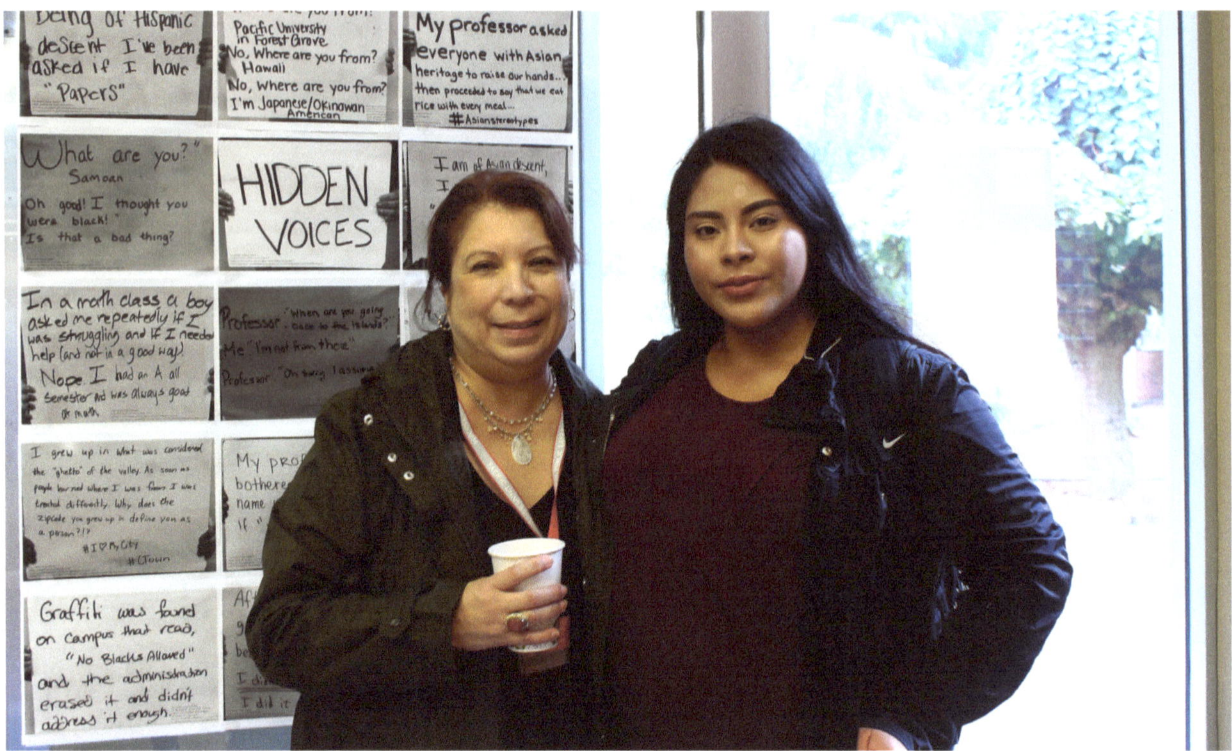

organization on campus, up and running. "We're still in infrastructure mode," she explains, but with the help of nine student leaders, she's working to get connected with all the Senates, Centers, and departments on campus. She wants to unify Pacific around clear goals that everyone knows and works together to create and that is what she hopes for in the future for the Pacific Family.

"Every family has a different way of running a family. You might have a family that dinners at six and everybody sits at the table and then you're gonna talk about your day… But you may have a family where the mom is out working two jobs and to have dinner is to just make sure that you have food to eat…It's the same at Pacific. Can we all sit down and have a conversation and program times or do we just have these random conversations outside of the classroom?"

Narce wants to embrace the different communities that exist on campus and unite them. Her visions of equity and inclusion require collaboration across campus, but she sees this as an attainable goal. It will just require the Pacific Family to work together day to day, as it takes time to understand different perspectives, and practice to implement change. This monumental task doesn't appear to phase her. She tells me confidently, "I am a little bit of everything because everything should have equity."

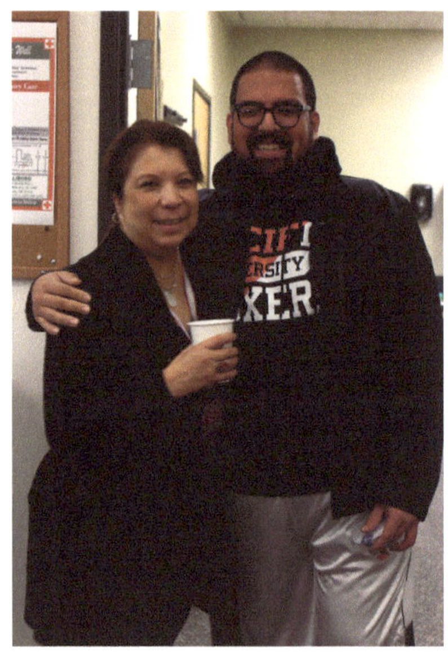

Despite her dedication to it, Narce's job isn't her whole life. She loves to spend time with her family, especially her two grandkids, Marques and Tommy. Proudly, she shows me

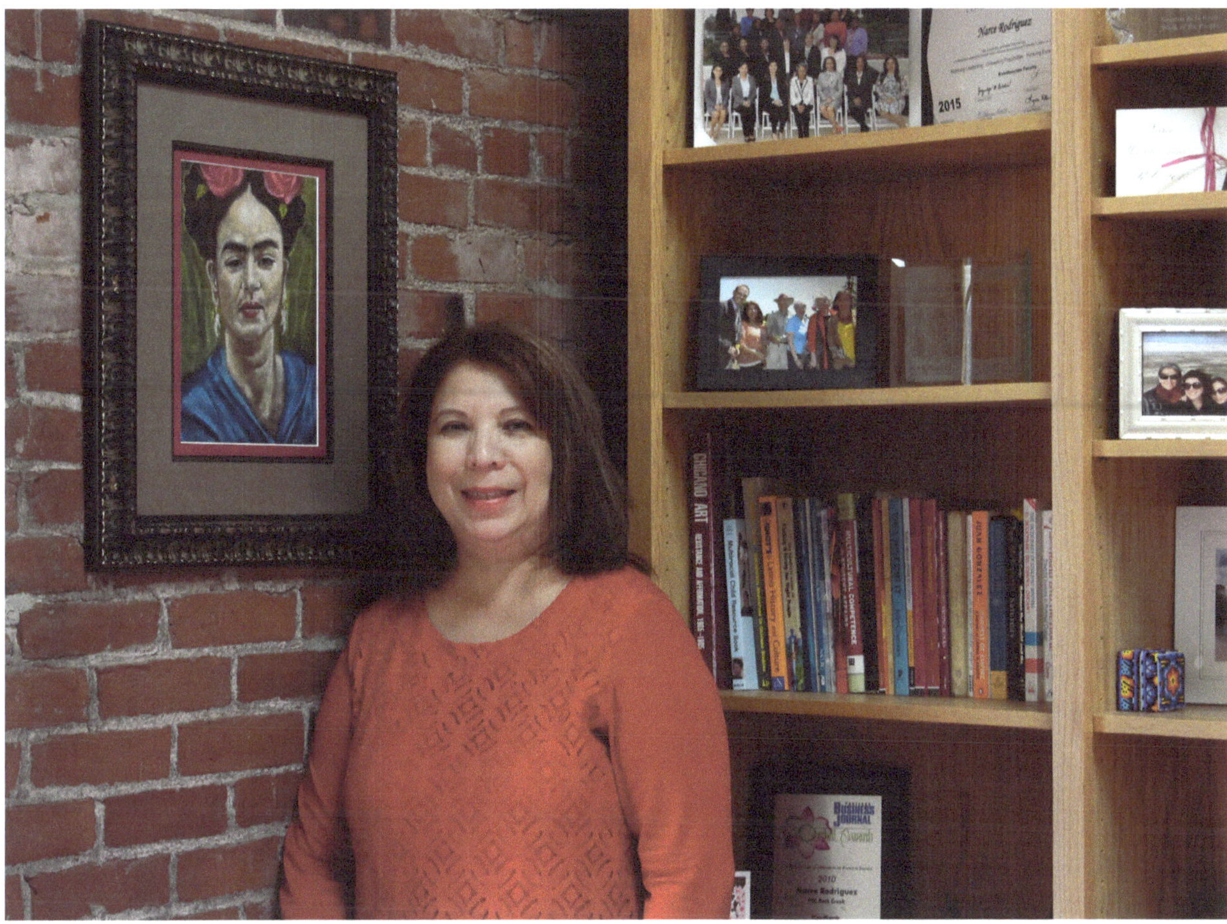

photos of nine month old Tommy, and laments the fact that twelve year old Marques never lets her take photos of him. She goes on to tell me, "I love to spend time with my family. I have a big family and the babies that are all being born. I have a whole bunch of nieces and nephews that are starting to have babies so that's fun."

When she's not in the thick of her large family, she likes her solitude to recharge. "I like just moments alone. I'm more of an introverted person, so I enjoy just looking out the window at birds and enjoying nature." In addition to her home life, her dedication to empowerment in her community is highlighted by her active involvement with Adelante Mujeres and Central Cultural. She negotiated a partnership between Pacific University and these organizations for DACA vigils this October.

As I leave Narce's office of warm smiles and laughter, I cannot help but think how brave and generous this woman really is. She came from hardship most students at Pacific have never experienced or had to imagine and made herself into an inspiring woman who has dedicated her life to making herself and her community a better place.

She is very new to the Pacific Family, but her passion for its growth and success is palpable. There doesn't seem to be a doubt in her mind that we can make the campus a more inclusive place for all students, faculty, staff, and the community—we're all a part of this family.

MIKE SHINGLE

narrative by Patrick Lagier
photographs by Dominic Sampaulesi

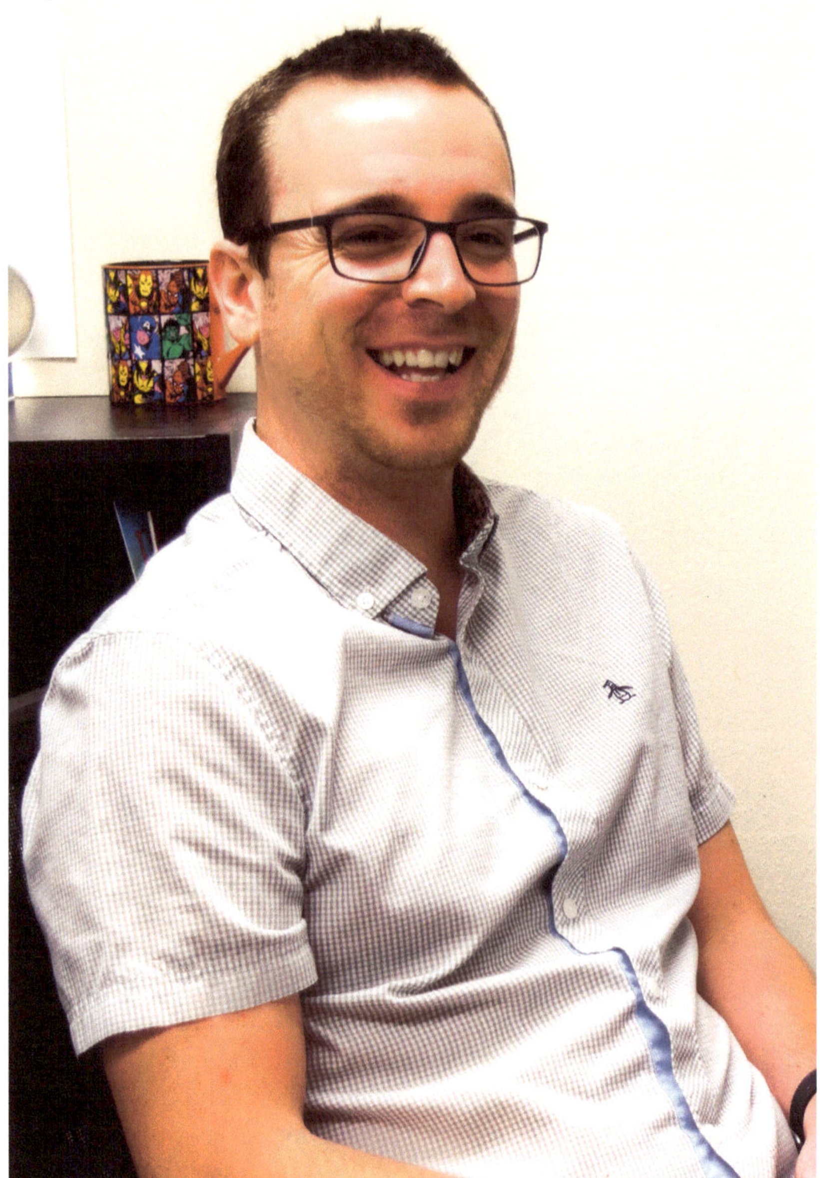

"Watch your head! We get a lot of basketball players with these low ceilings," Mike Shingle chuckles as we move into the basement of Bates House, a victorian house nestled between verdant trees and mossy bricks. Mike's office is a safe space for all students, nestled in a nook around a few sharp corners from the stairs, decorated with inspiring quotes and nerdy touches like a marvel calendar, an Avenger's coffee mug, and an Oregon local 'Hillsboro Hops' lunchbox. I casually ask about his work, and he laughs and retorts that he's "knee deep" in focal studies, a set of academic requirements for undergraduate students at Pacific University. As an adviser, his job is to help students plan personalized schedules to ensure they graduate as fast as is possible.

"My heart is with the transfer students," he explains, "because I went to community college, and worked as an advisor at P.C.C for a number of years, I understand both sides of it." He wants to set reasonable expectations for those students and ensure that they take the classes they need to graduate in the time they have. He focuses on time management and spacing out the workload in a realistic manner so that students, and especially student athletes don't burn out too soon into their academic career.

"You can't win them all," Mike explains. Students come in with a lot of credits that don't transfer and still expect to graduate in two years, but because of Pacific's prerequisite or mandatory class requirements, Mike must often break the news to them that it's going to be

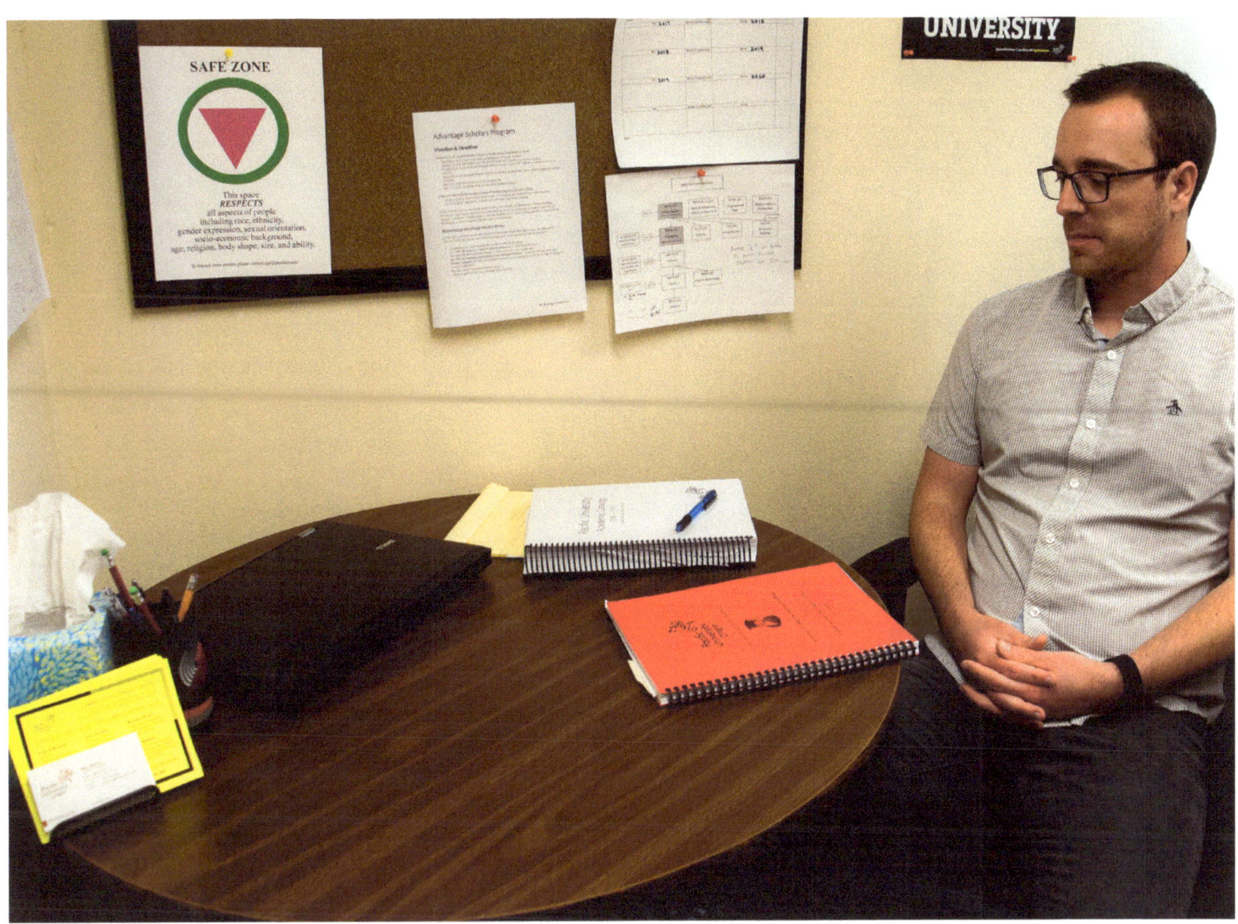

more than two years to graduate. If a student has failed a class or has issues with attendance, it can be many years, possibly more than they can afford. Mike does as much as he can to help those students, but only some requirements can be waived. However, despite the occasional outlier, the majority of students find a good (or at least decent) schedule that works for them.

Outside of work, Mike is a devoted sports fan having played basketball, baseball, football and soccer in school as well as regularly attending games with his wife, who he met while she was attending Oregon State University. He's most

> "My heart is with the transfer students because I went to community college…I understand both sides of it."

proud of his newfound ability to "adult," given that he's now coming up on his one year "workaversary," has consistently made his house payments, married his wife, and is about to become a proud father.

True to his office decor, he's also a nerd, the beaming owner of a retro video game collection (all classic titles of the 80's and 90's, with a flair for Zelda). His favorite superhero? "No contest," he says immediately "Iron-Man, for his whimsical nature and his wit, like when the first movie came out? I mean, come on!

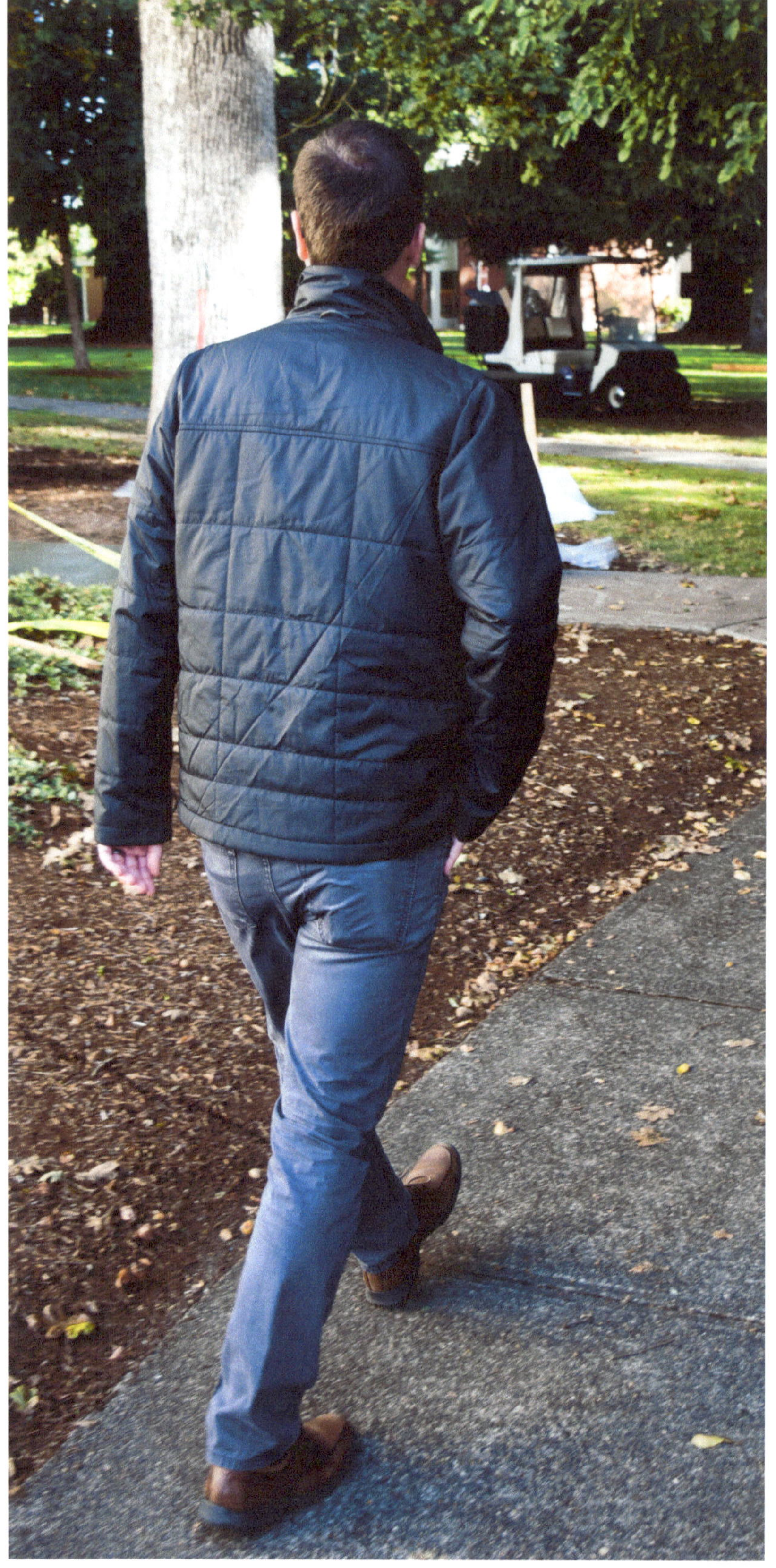

So cool." Although he didn't read the original comic books, he claims to have made up for it with the time he invested playing their spin-off video games when he was younger.

Growing up in eastern Oregon and then later moving to the greater Portland area, Mike recalls his childhood ambitions. Early in his college career he had focused on Pharmacy, wanting to follow in his mother's footsteps. However, a series of conversations with his academic adviser changed his mind. He realized he did not want to process death and grieving as closely as his mother had through her job as a pharmacist, but he did still want to help as many people as he could. Listening to both his own personal needs as well as his adviser's recommendation, Mike changed paths to focus on student aid, earning degrees in Biology and Spanish before graduating with a master's degree in collegiate student services. Now he remembers the conversations he was having with his adviser when he was a student "in need of having his head screwed on straight" and hopes that he can be that same guiding force for the newest generations of college students.

Mike Shingle | *The People Behind the Scenes of Pacific University*

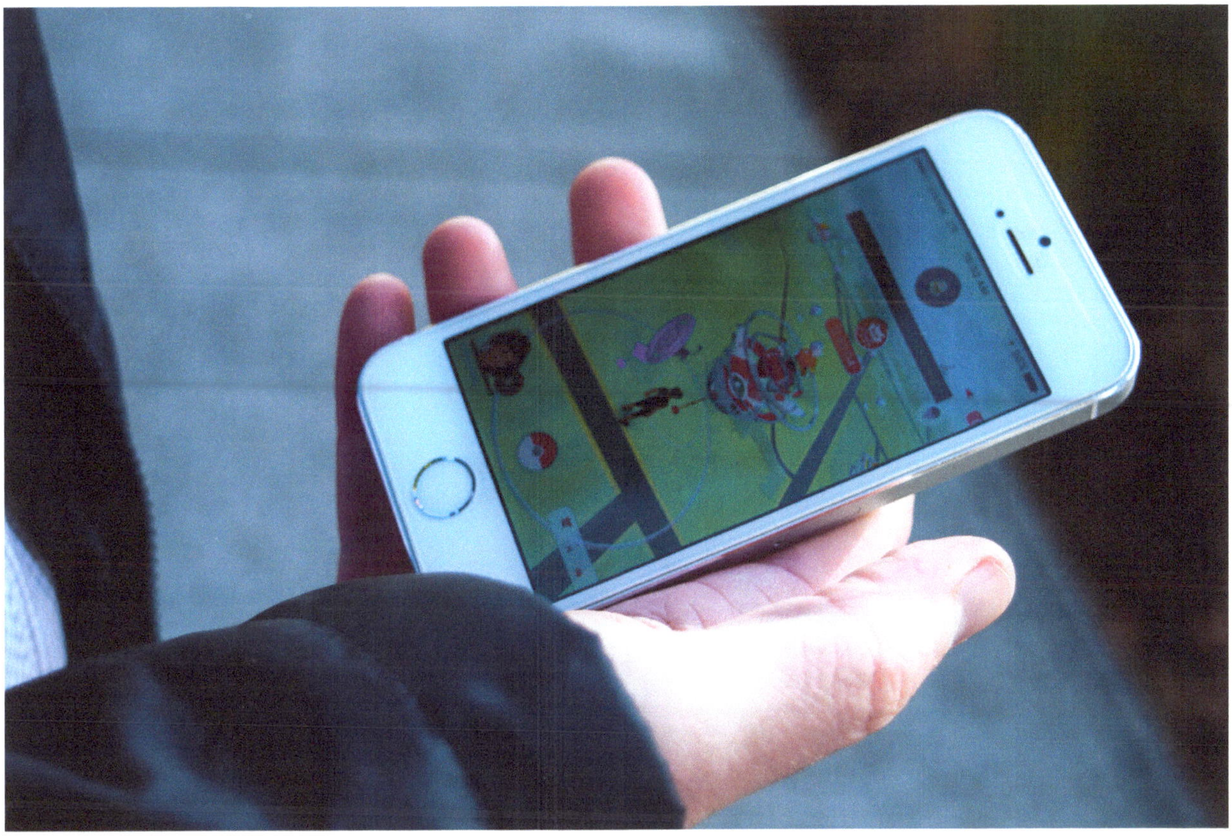

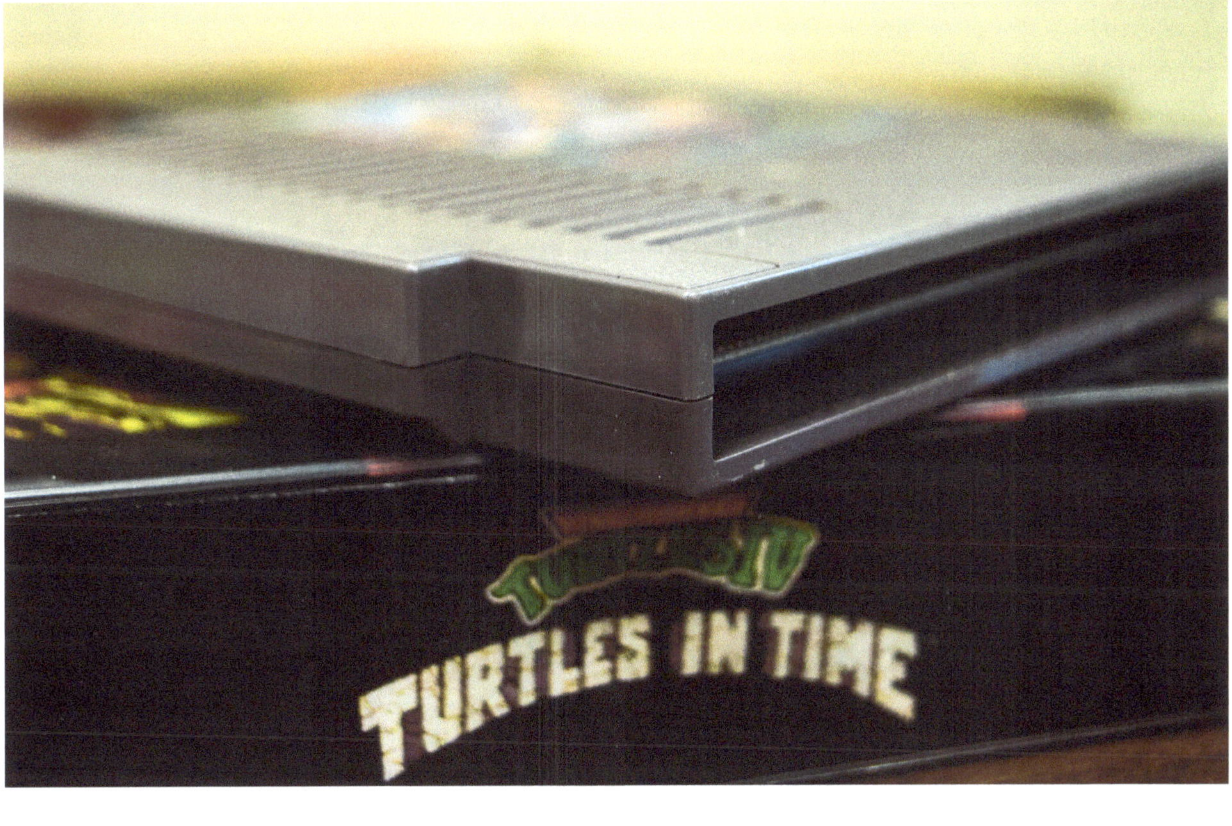

TURTLES IV
TURTLES IN TIME

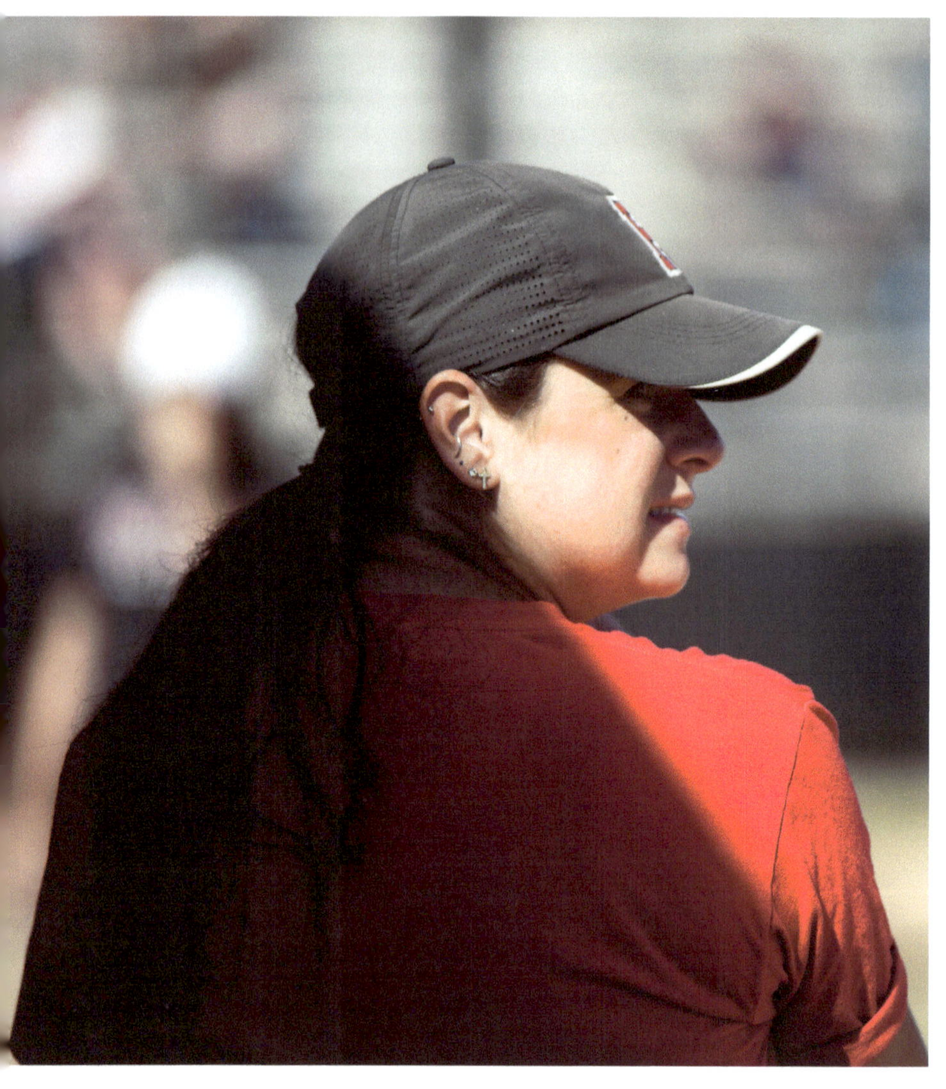

LIZ YANDALL

narrative by Julia Thomson
photographs by Tanner Boyle

Bats crack on softballs, teamates cry, "Yeah, girl!" after a particularly good hit. The smell of raindrops on grass drifts through the field.

Liz Yandall stands on the neatly combed field, with dirt already kicked up on her sneakers. She laughs with an entourage of assistant coaches and friends while watching her athletes hard at work, her arms folded over her very pregnant belly.

Practice is the softball coach's favorite part of the day, tied with any other time she's interacting with her players, other student athletes, or coaches. The Pacific community is important to her, she says, because "the more I get to know faculty, staff and professors, the more I'm able to help figure out how to best serve these kids at the end of the day." There is a joy in service for Liz. Whether she's encouraging her athletes, correcting their form, or organizing their events, Liz is happiest when she's helping somebody grow.

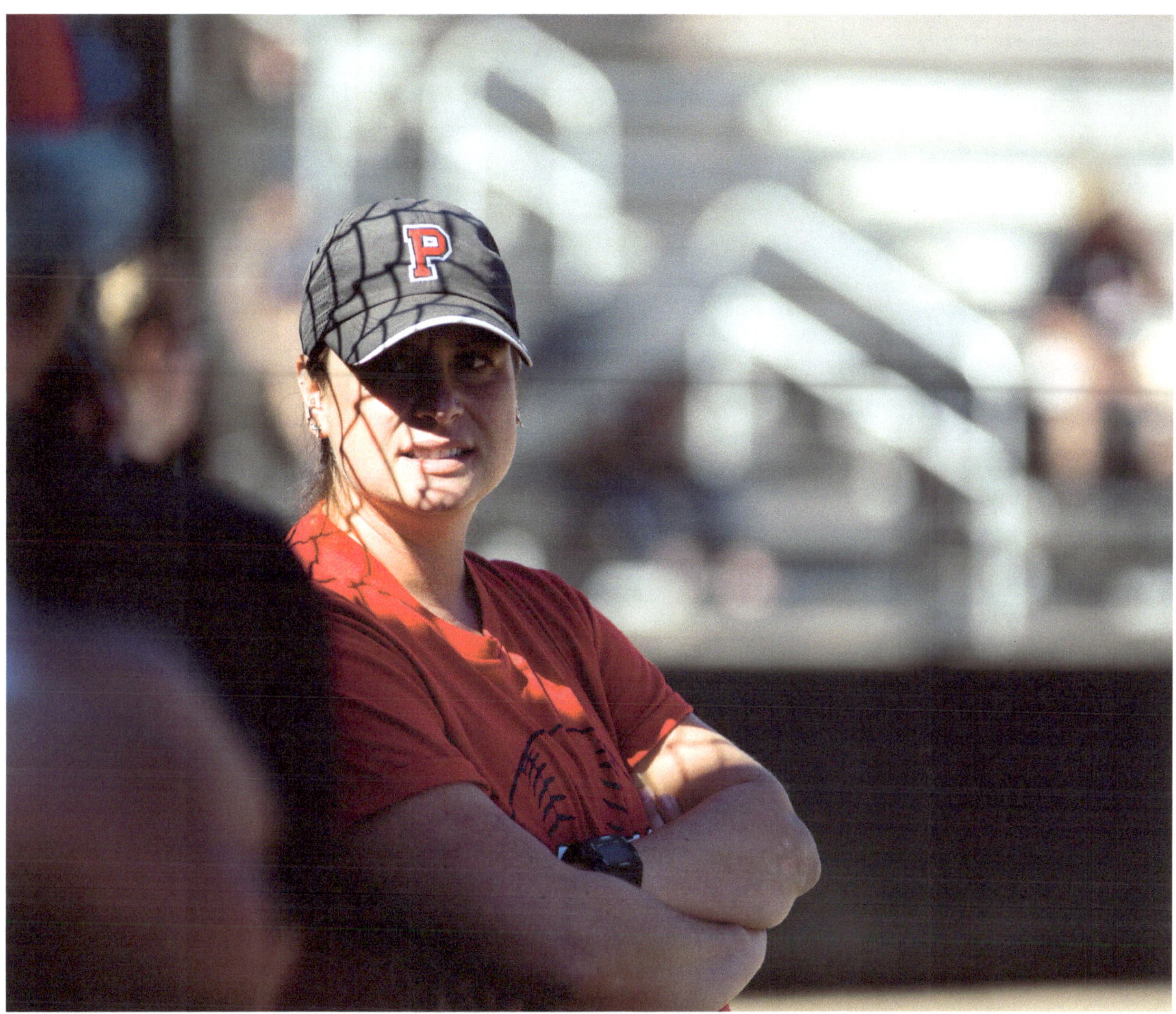

Being the adviser of the Fellow-ship of Christian Athletes is another opportunity for Liz to encourage growth in her students. The student club combines physical and spiritual strength, two things that are mean-ingful for Liz. She loves advising this club because it allows her to connect with student athletes from all sports and backgrounds. As important as sports are, there's nothing like meet-ing somebody new and having a conversation about life as a whole.

"One of the great things about coaching at Pacific is we're a small liberal arts school and we have such a diverse set of backgrounds that all come together, and I love that."

Liz doesn't measure her success in wins or losses, but according to people she can help. "Sports is so much more than just sports. Do I want to win? Absolutely. Are we aiming to win the conference cham-pionship while we're here? Yes! We

are going to figure out a way to make that happen. But to get to those levels, you have to teach them so many things that can help them off the field." What makes a good athlete is a supportive coach, and it's hard to think of somebody who cares more for her players than Liz.

Considering how dedicated to soft-ball she is, it's surprising to learn that she started her career at a market research firm. "I loved it. I got to

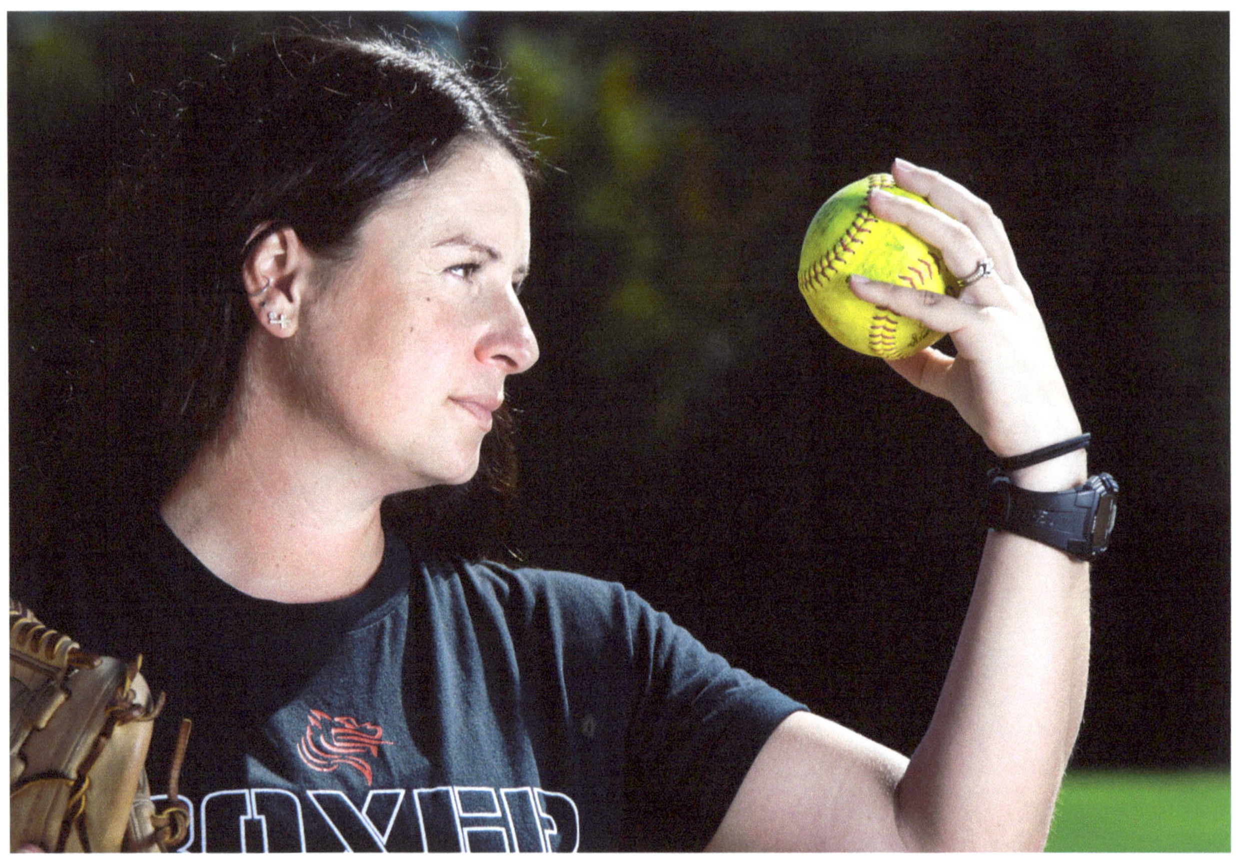

work some really high-profile clients and all that, but I could never leave the softball field." Her friend and former boss, Tim Hill, once asked her why she was still coaching soft-

"My heart's on the field...I just can't leave it."

ball if her market research job was so successful. Her answer was: "My heart's on the field, like I just can't leave it. And softball is so much more fulfilling to me than anything else, that I just had to stay."

From a young age, she learned about softball and coaching by watching her father. It isn't his games that she remembers, but the influence he had on his athletes. "My parents opened their doors to anybody. If a wrestler had a bad home life and needed a spot to crash for a little bit, they'd crash on our couch, or we had a softball player that would come by and get breakfast before school every day. Just being able to see them have a positive impact on student athletes was deeper than I knew. It was one of the reasons I couldn't walk away from the field."

Today, sports of all kinds are a family bonding experience. "Most family gatherings are around current coaching positions. We'll all come tailgate for Lukkes' football game, or they'll come out for a softball game. Sports are definitely a part of our everyday lives." You can even find her family around Pacific, as her Dad helps Liz with practice and her brother is Lukkes Gilgan, the Defensive Coordinator of Pacific's football team. Liz says, "I love that it's kind of a family affair at Pacific right now." That family is preparing to welcome a new addition, since Liz and her husband are expecting their first child at any moment. Liz feels excited about her son. "I know this little guy is going to grow up with so many people who love and care about him. He's already so

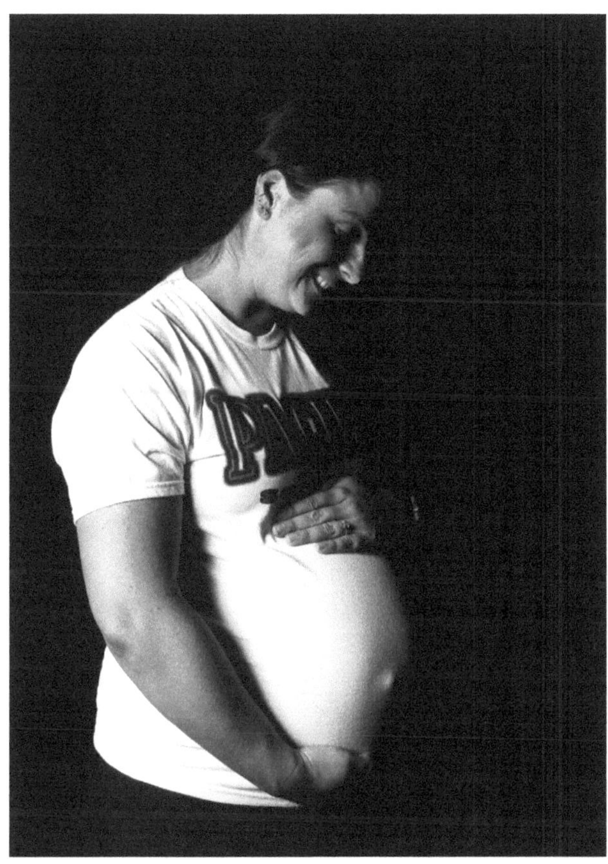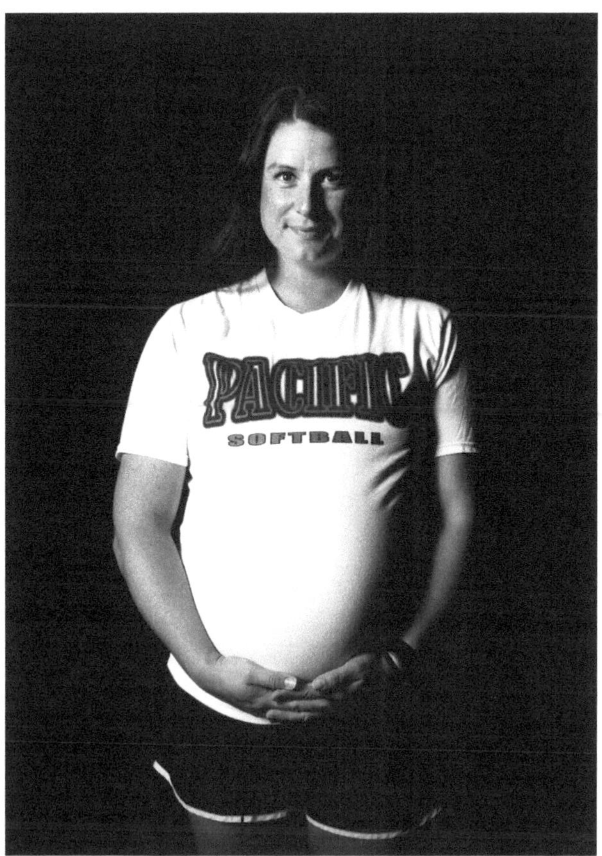

loved, it's exciting to bring him into the world that way."

It may be surprising to learn that in addition to her lifelong interest in sports, Liz has always been very academically minded. Through hard work and dedication that is typical of Liz, she earned her bachelor's degree from Willamette University in three years, then went on to earn a master's degree early, too. "I was a total nerd growing up, not in a bad way. People tend to be surprised by that, I think they think I'm more jock-minded when they meet me." This is further proven by the Wolverine figurine living on her desk. She likes Hugh Jack-man's interpretation of the character, although her husband's opinion differs. In whatever part of life Liz tackles, be it softball or superheroes, she does so with a strong, but humble, sense of self.

When the team finishes warm-ups, they huddle together before the official start of practice. Liz is in the center, surrounded by her girls. In a strong voice, she reads a quote from *Chase the Lion* by Mark Batterson. "When the London Philharmonic Orchestra selected the fifty greatest pieces of classical music, the list included... three by Bach... Bach wrote more than a thousand pieces of music. If it had been base-ball, Bach would have been batting a .003! Total failure, right? Wrong! That might not seem like a great batting average, but it takes lots of swings to get a hit…We glamorize success, but it always comes back to basics." For Liz Yandall, the basics are where her heart is: softball, family, and faith.